# THE POETRY AND LIFE OF
# ALLEN GINSBERG

# THE POETRY AND LIFE OF ALLEN GINSBERG

### A NARRATIVE POEM

## EDWARD SANDERS

THE OVERLOOK PRESS
WOODSTOCK & NEW YORK

First published in the United States in 2000 by
The Overlook Press, Peter Mayer Publishers, Inc.
Lewis Hollow Road
Woodstock, New York 12498
www.overlookpress.com

Library of Congress Cataloging-in-Publication Data

Sanders, Edward.
The poetry and life of Allen Ginsberg; a narrative poem/Edward Sanders.
p.  cm.
Includes bibliographical references (p.245).
1. Ginsberg, Allen, 1926—Poetry. 2. Poets, American—Poetry.
3. Beat generation—Poetry. 4. Poetics— Poetry.  I. Title
PS3569.A49 P64 2000     811'54—dc21     00-26619

Type formatting by Bernard Schleifer Company
Manufactured in the United States of America
FIRST EDITION
1 3 5 7 9 8 6 4 2
ISBN 1-58567-037-5

Dedicated to building of
the civilization envisioned by
Allen Ginsberg in such poems as "America":

*When can I go into the supermarket and buy what I need*
*with my good looks?*

and "Death to Van Gogh's Ear!":

*Now is the time for prophecy without death as a consequence*

and "Memory Gardens":

*Well, while I'm here I'll*
*do the work—*
*and what's the Work?*
*To ease the pain of living.*
*Everything else, drunken*
*dumbshow.*

# PART I

## 1926–1943

In a way Allen Ginsberg's life was
shaped by pogroms and the surge of
revolution
        in the Jewish Pale of Settlement

first in the 1880s
and then in the pogrom-evil years of '03-'05
                which caused his grandparents on both sides
                to flee to the freedom of the USA


## THE PALE

The Pale was the legal zone in western Russia
set up through the centuries
        where almost 5 million Jews
                were forced to reside

The Pale extended from the Baltic Sea in the north
to the Black Sea in the south.
In the 19th century it included Lithuania,
Belorussia (White Russia), the Crimea
                Bessarabia & much of the Ukraine.

## GRANDPARENTS IN THE PALE

Allen Ginsberg's grandfather Pincus was born in a town called
Kamenetz-Podolskiy on the upper Dniester River
He was orphaned early,
then moved to Pinsk further north in the Pale

There were ghastly new restrictions on Jews in 1881

in the repression after the assassination of Tzar Alexander II
and many instances of government-sanctioned pogroms.
The Tzar even banned the Yiddish Theater
and restrictions were increased on where Jews
                              could live in the Pale.
There were quotas set up on the number of Jews
to be let into the universities,
                    and to legal, medical and government jobs.

It was in this context that Pincus Ginsberg fled to the USA
                                        in the 1880s
to settle with relatives in Newark, where he met his future bride
Rebecca Schechtman--
Louis Ginsberg, Allen's father, was born in '95

## HIS MATERNAL GRANDFATHER
## & GRANDMOTHER

Mendel Livergant
was Naomi's father
(changed to Morris Levy at Ellis Island)

& lived in a village named Nevel
south of St. Petersburg, west of Moscow
& north of Vitebsk
          in the middle of the Jewish Pale
where he sold Singer sewing machines to the peasants

Mendel married a woman named Judith
they had four children,
          all of whom wound up in Allen's poems–
Eleanor, Max, Sam & Naomi
                who was born in 1894

Naomi grew up speaking Yiddish
She played the mandolin
Her parents were sympathetic
                to the revolutionaries.

          In the Russo-Japanese war of 1904
          Mendel Livergant and his bro' Isser
          went to the U.S.
                    to avoid getting drafted

(& underwent the name change
             from Livergant to Levy)

& Judith & the kids
moved to Vitebsk
             a city of radical ferment
(where Marc Chagall
             had lived when young)

–Vitebsk was later destroyed by the Nazis.

Then there was
what they called the Revolution of 1905
when the Tzar's soldiers opened fire
on 300,000 marchers petitioning for
             the 8-hour workday, more money, the
                   right to vote & a parliament
             & 100 protesters,
some praying and carrying ikons
fell dead in the snow
             by the Winter Palace
after which
there were massive strikes in cities
                   all over Russia,
             and then massive repression
             including ghastly pogroms
                   in the northern Pale

–pogrom is the Russian word for "devastation"

This was the year that
Naomi, age 10, & her mother and sisters
escaped to New York
             to Orchard Street

(Isser's family went to Winnipeg)

& her father Morris opened a candy store
in the Lower East Side

Then the family moved to Newark
Naomi went to Barringer High
in 1912
where, both age 17, she met Louis Ginsberg.

## ONE SOCIALIST, ONE COMMUNIST

Allen's mother was a communist

Louis was a socialist like his parents

& thus was established a
classic pull-&-shove
in the family
         'tween the two sets of politics

## NAOMI'S FIRST BREAKDOWN

Naomi had gone to Normal School
& become a teacher
        in Woodbine, NJ

She suffered her first breakdown in 1919
   light was painful to her
   she lay in a dark room 3 weeks
   She was not yet married
   but later that year, with the opposition of
   her future mother-in-law
   she and Louis were hitched

The first son, Eugene, was born 1921
and named after the great American Socialist
                       Eugene Debs

## THE BARD

The bard named Irwin Allen Ginsberg
was born at 2 A.M. on June 3, 1926
                in Newark, NJ
They named him after
    his great-grandfather
        S'rul Avrum Ginsberg

Louis was an English teacher
    at Central High in Paterson

He was a well-known poet
    with three volumes published during his lifetime

"Would that all sons' fathers were poets!"
A.G. later exclaimed, in his "Confrontation with Louis
Ginsberg's Poems" in  Louis Ginsberg's
                                        *Collected Poems.*

          An early family apartment was
                          on Fair Street in Paterson
          now torn down
          not far from the Great Falls
                          in the Passaic River

          where Louis sat
                  in the evenings
                  at a modest wooden desk
          'neath a gooseneck lamp
                          writing poetry
          –a desk that Allen later acquired
                  after his father's passing in '76
          and brought to his apartment
                          in the Lower East Side

      Allen wrote a poem when he was nine or ten
      which was published in the *Paterson Evening News*
      He could still recall it 60 years later:

              "Once upon my window sill
              A sparrow hopped but then stood still
              I asked him why he did the latter
              He said to me, 'It doesn't matter.'
              Men kill a cow for mutton pie
              So should I confide in you my woe?"

      Allen, his brother and mother spent
      two summers at Camp Nicht-Gedeiget
      which means "No Worry"
                      near Monroe Lake
                          in Orange County
                              about 60 miles north of
              New York City  (Louis wd visit on weekends)

              Allen's first songs were
              learned at his mom's communist meetings:
              "On the Line" &
              "The Red Flag"

Around 1929
after Naomí had pancreas surgery
she flipped again--
Light and sound hurt her
She was sent to Bloomingdale Sanatorium
                            not far from Tarrytown

   Around 6 months later
   she was let out
   and joined the family in Paterson--
   1930

### 1935

1935, Naomi another session with flip
again light gave her great pain
After two months she came out of it

Then a few months later,
either late '35 or early '36,
she went under again
and was sent to Greystone and
given shock treatments

Naomi returned home in '36

Naomi more paranoid
Was sent back to sanatorium on June 24
She was there three years (Greystone)
and let out in 1939

### 1940

He was an early "Jack the Clipper"
an attribute that remained
                        throughout his life

as he amassed many many many news clippings
on Hitler and Mussolini, and the Spanish Civil War.
in the late '30s into 1940

He learned of his gayness apparently by high school time
but kept many locks on the door
He wrote his class graduation poem
& wondered which college to attend

He leaned toward Columbia
to follow a friend from Paterson High

He kept getting crushes on fellow students
One student, Paul Roth, went to Columbia
later became a doctor
    Allen kept his crush in secrecy

## 1942

Naomi was again hospitalized at Greystone
         in '42 and '43.

## PART II

## 1943

*The Vow to Help the Working Class*

The slender & nervous sixteen-year-old
took the ferry from Hoboken to Manhattan
on the way to the university entrance examination
and made a solemn vow
that if he got into Columbia
he would devote his life
      to helping the working class

(Ginsberg was prone to vows--
    see his later vows with Neal Cassady
    and Peter Orlovsky)

He enrolled at Columbia in '43, age 16
an Ivy League school—hardly a citadel of sentiment
for the workers
    even with ex-radicals like Lionel Trilling
    and Marxist art-genius Meyer Schapiro
        as his mentors

That was the school year
he met young Republican Jack Kerouac
and continued his fierce training in rhyme

(He forged beautiful skills at rhyme
to which he returned toward the end of his life.
He was famous throughout his career for his
spontaneous rhymes)

Among his faves were Thomas Wyatt &
Christopher Smart  (1722-1771)
whose "Jubilate Agno"
was written while Smart was crazed.

Ginsberg
with a crazy mother
was very very sensitive
to
craziness
Crazy Wisdom
Crazy Times
& Vision

Another big influence, of course, was
Walt Whitman, Ginsberg's lifelong "unwobbling pivot"
described by him in a letter to one of his college professors as
a "Mountain too vast to be seen."

Decades later, when reading from Whitman to his students,
he would weep during "When Lilacs Last in the Dooryard Bloom'd."

And so Irwin Allen Ginsberg began
a polite, Cold War liberal Columbia upbringing--

In December o' '43 he met one William S. Burroughs
who was working as a bartender in the Village
His parents, who operated a gift shop and
garden supply shop in Fla., sent him $200 a month--

Ginsberg & Kerouac
learned much from Burroughs' library
Ginsberg first experienced Blake there,
and Baudelaire
Big impact on future Beats:
Burroughs' Book Hoard

Another lifelong friend A.G. met his first year in college
was Lucien Carr, a polished & confident youth from St. Louis
whom Allen first saw in Lionel Trilling's Great Books seminar

## 1944

Naomi had been released from Greystone
& Allen often went with her to the opera

Louis & Naomi broke up that year
Her paranoia & all the fights
                    were finally too much for both to endure
Naomi moved to NYC
          where she had a love affair with a doctor
          for the National Maritime Union
                              & lived with him for a while.
          Around May of '44
          the 'Zap* met Kerouac
          who was then a merchant seaman
          (it was World War II)
                              apparently at the pad of
                              Edie Parker and Joan Vollmer
                              on 118th Street
          (the crowd hung out at the nearby West End Bar)

          Kerouac flunked out of Columbia in '42
          In December '42 he joined the navy, but then feigned
                              bonk bonk to get a discharge
          then joined the merchant marines.

          Ginsberg and K. were talking buddies

          On August 14, Lucien Carr killed David Kammerer
          Burroughs' pal from St. Louis
                              who was erotically obsessed with
                                        the attractive young man

          —late at night, in Riverside Park, Upper West Side of
          Manhattan
                              knifed him twice in the heart

---

*I often referred to my longtime pal as Ginzap or just 'Zap.

tied up the body & rolled it in the Hudson River

Burroughs gave Carr some cash and some advice
Kerouac helped dispose of the death knife
                              and Kammerer's glasses

●

Through Burroughs, Kerouac and Ginzap
discovered uppers, particularly benzedrine
                    available in drugstores in inhalers
an important force
          in Kerouac's novels
                    and Ginsberg's poems

& in the forging of literary frenzy

●

August 16 Carr turned himself in
          confessed, charged with murder

Burroughs and Kerouac were arrested
& Kerouac's father refused to bail him out.

Jack was taken from jail to marry Edie Parker

Then, freed on bail, they went to live in
                    Grosse Point, Mich. for a while
                              —a brief while

## 1945

3-16-45 a Columbia U dean
rushed into Ginzap's room at the college
and found him in bed with Kerouac
(they had on shorts)
sleeping

Allen had written "Fuck the Jews" with accompanying
skull and crossbones on the window,

putatively to miff the reportedly antiSemitic
cleaning woman.
Ginzap had also written on the glass
     "Butler has no balls" (Butler was one of the
          college's deans)

A.G. had to wipe off the words
and was suspended from college
    ordered to see a shrink
      and tossed from the residence
for having the unwelcome overnight guest (Kerouac)
& for the graffiti

A.G. later told his biographers he was trying to goad
          the antisem cleaner

## A YEAR FROM COLLEGE

After this, age 18,
he took a year from college

    He worked first as a welder at
        Brooklyn Navy Yard, till April
then at Gotham Book Mart, but
      owner Frances Steloff fired him.

June of '45 he received his draft notice.
    Hitler was dead &
    Hiroshima a few weeks ahead
He declared himself homosexual
was sent to merchant marine training school
      for rest of summer of '45

Beginning in August
    he was in U.S. Maritime
    Service for 3 1/2 months

During '45 Kerouac's father dying of C
and Jack spent lots of time at home

Ginsberg and Jack
began talking about the "New Vision"

early urgings that lead to the B.G.

Ginsberg fell in love with Kerouac
Down in gay part of Manhattan, by th'
west side docks,
they caressed one another

## 1946

Naomi living with Eugene, who was out of
        the WWII army & off to law school
She was prone to stride around nude
A.G. apparently felt his mom's nudity
reinforced his gayness

      (see Ginsberg's poem "Kaddish")

In th' fall of '46, Ginzap readmitted to Columbia

Same fall Kerouac was living in Ozone Park (in NYC)
working on *The Town and the City.*

& Lucien Carr was let out after two years
for the Kammerer killing

Ginsberg was in constant communication with his father,
        often by card and mail
        The correspondence was often
        what they call brutally direct

Fall of '46 Neal Cassady to NYC with
17-year-old wife LuAnne
Cassady was from the flophouse realm of
                   Denver

## 1947

January, Ginsberg met the youth from Denver

Cassady was already a friend of Jack Kerouac
A.G. and Cassady made it first
on a cot in a Harlem pad
          in January '47

March, Cassady split back to Denver

Summer Kerouac and Ginsberg joined him there

>Ginzap went to Denver
>to be with Cassady
>Cassady was very involved with
>>girlfriend Carolyn
>--also seeing first wife, and
>various others, plus furtively
>making it with A.G.

>Ginsberg frustrated,
>wrote fairly good poem on August 23
>>"The Bricklayer's Lunch"

writing rhymed quatrains on benzedrine
the summer o' '47 in Denver

>Hitching ca end of August 47
>with Cassady toward Burroughs'
>grass ranch
>>in New Waverly, Texas

>they took a vow of love and fidelity
>kneeling together in Oklahoma
>(as mentioned in "The Green Automobile")

Ginsberg dropped out of Columbia again, and after summer
took merchant ship to Africa and back

Then rest of fall worked odd jobs in Paterson

Winter to pad in East Harlem

In the Milieu of Aimless Frenzy

>Naomi moved in with her sister Edie
>who worked days as a union organizer.
>Naomi getting crazy
>>fearful of relatives with bags
>>of germs
>>>on the fire escape
>or the "three big sticks" in her back
>1947  flipped again
>sent to Pilgrim State on Long Island

Hitting her head against wall
Docs recommended lobotomy
Allen signed forms okaying
                it in late Nov. 1947
(a source of some of his guilt)

I think she was there till she died
on June 9, 1956

## 1948

Winter of '47-'48, the 'Zap returned to Columbia
in a frenzy

Writing a paper on Cézanne
for Meyer Schapiro
he'd take some tokes
then go Cézanne-staring
at MOMA

On way back from a seder in Paterson
(at Louis' house)
Allen and Kerouac
parted at 125th Street.
Allen demanded Jack hit him--
"I wanted attention from him
                any kind of attention"

April Cassady wrote he was married, and wife
was pregnant

"Two Sonnets" after reading Kerouac's manuscript,
      *The Town and the City*   Spring of 1948

Serendipity
Allen's friend w/ tb
from whom he rented a pad w/

orange crate shelves
theology studies
St. Theresa of Avila
Plotinus
St. J of the C
        all material for "Howl"

Living in East Harlem-- June-July 1948:
where he had an auditory "vision"

heard a voice chanting Blake's "Ahh, Sunflower, Weary of Time"
and "The Sick Rose" and "Little Girl Lost."

(Out of that vision his early poem
"On Reading William Blake's 'The Sick Rose'")

### WATCH OUT, BARD

He crawled
        onto the fire escape
to the window next door
He tapped and shouted
"I've seen God!"
        to two startled women

## PART III

We left Allen Ginsberg in his East Harlem apartment
in the summer of '48
where he had experienced a powerful auditory "vision" of
the Bard William Blake chanting poetry

an experience that was to be key in Ginsberg's
next fifteen years as a poet.

Around this time Allen began inserting questions
into his poetry--
His very early works
contain few, if any,
bardic questions:
but when he gets to his
"Vision" poem:
        "On Reading William Blake's 'The Sick Rose,'"
written at the time of the Blake Voice Vision,

there are three sentences ending in question marks.

After the Vision of Blake, the Elegant, Pulsing Question
became one of his most powerful poetic devices

(There are 47 question marks in Allen's *Collected Poems*
in the poems BEFORE he wrote "Howl" in 1955)

> ("Howl" has no question marks
> because "Howl" is, in a way, the long declarative
> throb-answer to
> hundreds of questions he had already asked.)

In his Blake Vision, of course, he sensed Eternity
and it set off a long hunger to
"see Visionary Indian Angels who WERE Visionary Indian Angels"

(The next fifteen years were a quest for Cosmic Consciousness
up until his poem "The Change" written after experiencing
the Calcutta ghats
amoil with flame
--a poem renouncing the
"power" he had constructed out of
the Blake Vision)

The Blake Vision also had "Holy Loner" aspects
that brought into focus
his "feelings of rejection as a confessed homosexual
and as a Jew,"
as the writer Paul Christiansen has pointed out.

His father, Louis, watched his son with a wary eye:
July '48:
Louis' advice re Neal
"Dear Allen, Exorcise Neal.
--Louis"

## 1949

There came a time in February o' '49
when a bedraggled, Loner Beat, Famished Phantom
named Herbert Huncke showed up at A.G.'s pad
at 1401 York Avenue

just released from prison, feet blistered, socks wet
and talking suicide

He was the archetypal "Madman beat in time"
of the "Howl" threnody

Allen offered him a place to stay
Not long thereafter Huncke began bringing his pals to the pad

a heist gang
        that used the place for storage of stolen stuff

On April 23 all were arrested,
even the Bard Allen Ginsberg,

it made a big splash in *The New York Times:*

*One of the accused, Allen Ginsberg, of 1401 York Avenue
told the police that he was a copy boy for a news service who
had "tied-in" with the gang, all with police records, to obtain
"realism" he needed to write a story.*

Sure, Allen, sure.

A sad sad dad bailed out his son
Mark Van Doren, of the Columbia U faculty, offered help
and Lionel Trilling introduced the Bard to a Col. U law prof
who recommended that A.G. plead bonk bonk

Allen did just that
and was sentenced to Columbia Presbyterian Psychiatric Institute

There wasn't a room available right away
so he lived with his dad in Paterson

and then on 6-29-49

the up-a-creek Bard went into the 6th-floor ward of the
Institute on
168th Street

where he met poet Carl Solomon
        to whom he was to dedicate "Howl"

## PART IV

    We left the story of the great Bard Allen Ginsberg
    when he was in Columbia Presbyterian Psychiatric Center
    in Washington Heights

    after being swept up on the edges of a heist gang
    run by the future Beat hero,
        but then down and out, Herbert Huncke

—There was a car chase, with Ginsberg
   one of the occupants
        and a famous arrest that made the
        front page of *The New York Times*

Several professors at Columbia pulled strings,
as they say,

and Ginsberg entered the Washington Heights shrink zone
in late June of 1949--

He was very depressed

Then one day Ginsberg was standing in the hallway
watching a guy being wheeled into the ward

swollen from insulin shocks

and began one of the more famous of
20th-century literary conversations

He traced through his visionary experiences
       (the Voice of Blake in Harlem '48 for instance)

The man listened exceptionally unimpressed, then said,
"Well, you're new here. Wait a while and you'll meet
some of the other repentant mystics."

The man asked who Ginsberg was. "I'm Myshkin,"
Allen replied, referring to the rather crazy prince in
Dostoyevsky's *The Idiot.*

The bloat-faced man then said, "I'm Kirilov," referring
to a character in *The Possessed.*

The shock patient was Carl Solomon, to whom the Bard was to
dedicate "Howl" five years later.

A talented writer, Solomon was living proof to Ginsberg
that the best minds of his generation were
                  destroyed by madness.

Solomon had once seen a performance in Paris by
Artaud himself

and on another famous occasion
had thrown potato salad at
    a lecturer speaking on "Stéphane Mallarmé
       and Alienation"
          at Brooklyn College

immortalized later in "Howl."

    Ginsberg wrote William Burroughs from the
    institute and said he was again thinking
    of becoming a labor lawyer

    Burroughs wrote back in a disquieting mood:
    "I think the US is heading
    in the direction of a
    socialist police state
    similar to England, &
    not too different from
    Russia.  I congratulate myself
    on my timely withdrawal."

### 1950

    2-27-50
    'Zap
    left the
    nuthouse
        & moved in w/ Dad
        in Paterson

He was convinced, at that moment,
that the best course for his life
was to find a job, get a girlfriend, return to Paterson.

He told Jack Kerouac his days of being gay were over

    Five days later Ginsberg sent 9 poems to the
    great William Carlos Williams

    (having just seen Williams read at the Guggenheim Museum)

    including "Ode to the Setting Sun," a New Jersey industrial
    landscape graveyard poem
    (written in the Psychiatric Institute)
    which predicted the great "Sunflower Sutra" o' 1955

The Letter to WCW
with 9 poems, and several other verses
form the text of the small collection known as
*The Gates of Wrath*, which was later
lost for many years, it seems, and was only
able to be published when Bob Dylan
found it in his archives around 1968

*The Gates of Wrath*'s themes are "passionate love and
the divided self." Plus, of course, thanatopsis

No other Bard since Poe has so delved death.

Ginsberg once told me what an influence Poe was
on his poesy.

The thanatopoesis opted early, as in
"In Death, Cannot Reach What Is Most Near"  &
"This Is About Death"
                    both from mid-1949

The first version of "The Shrouded Stranger"
was in *The Gates of Wrath*

              "The Shrouded Stranger"
              to me
              is his first poem
              to match the pulses of his psyche

                    ●

        In the spring of '50
        in Provincetown
true to his promise to the psychiatrists
he had his first heterosexual love
            an out-of-door bliss-zap by the docks

with a woman named Helen Parker
who had once been engaged to John Dos Passos
They fell in love
but he was not willing to leave Paterson & his therapy
for life with her in P-town
and a few months later she set aside Ginzap
for a singer named Ramblin' Jack Elliott!!

That was the spring he was hired as a reporter
for a labor newspaper, *Labor Herald,*
                                in New Jersey

but he was fired in September

then decided he'd go on prole-patrol with a job in a
ribbon factory in Paterson.

Meanwhile his father Louis
had married a woman from Paterson named Edith
& Louis & Edith had purchased a house.

Always a family man
            Allen & Edith were close over the years
& Edith was pleasantly tolerant
                        of the young men soon
                        to form a Generation

### 1951

Meanwhile in '51
Williams put two of Ginsberg's letters into the fourth
book of *Paterson,* published that year

and in the spring in an apartment on West 20th
across from a seminary
Jack Kerouac wrote *On the Road*
            cooked for and coddled by his wife Joan Haverty

That summer she was pregnant
            He insisted she have an abortion.  She refused.
                  And he dumped her
                              refusing to pay for the
                              prenatal doctor
                        & denying he was the father of
                        Jan Michelle Kerouac
                                    born on 2-16-52

From mid-'51 to the end of 1953
the 'Zap lived in NYC
preparing the manuscript for *Empty Mirror*   1947-'52

(which was not published till 1961)

## 1952

New Directions' James Laughlin
accepted some "prose poems" for publication.

## 1953

Good poem:
"The Green Automobile"  1953-1954

& in the summer
Ginzap worked as a copy boy
for the New York *Herald Tribune*
$45 a week

and almost every day
of these years he read torrentially
and asked 10,000s of questions
(Allen asked more questions, I think,
than anyone I ever met)

In late '53
to Florida to hang out w/ Wm Burroughs
then Havana, then Mexico

for a few months of many adventures.

## 1954

One of the adventures included
making himself some huge drums
suspended by vines
and tapping a rubber tree to tip his drumsticks

(See his poem "Siesta in Xbalba    Chiapas-SF")

That spring he split for California
to be with Neal Cassady

and lived for a while in an impossible
ménage à trois
with Neal and his wife Carolyn
He savored the quick and flaming literary scene:
Kenneth Rexroth, Robert Duncan, Jack Spicer, Kenneth Patchen

the year of Allen's great song
　　　　　"The Weight of the World is Love."

He moved to a pad on Nob Hill with a girlfriend, Sheila Boucher

and the 'Zap picked up a job for $250 a week
　　　　　　　　　doing market research

Then in December he met Peter Orlovsky
a friend of the painter Robert LaVigne
　　　　　　　　and they soon became lovers

Orlovsky came from a troubled impoverished family,
the third of five children
　　　　and had been on his own since age 17
He brought his brothers Julius & Lafcadio
　　　　　　　into the Beat milieu with him.
Both brothers were in and out of hospitals.
Julius once remained silent for 14 years,
　　　　(or so A.G. once told Ezra Pound & Olga Rudge)
in the mode of a Manichaean
because he felt that the entirety of evil in the cosmos
was coming from his mouth and body

### 1955

Ginsberg's
shrink
　　　　at Langley Porter
told A.G.

it was OK to
move in w/ Peter Orlovsky
give up his job
& write poetry

"I asked him what the
　　　　　American Psychoanalytic Association
wd say about that
& he said
　　　　'There's no party line
　　　　no red book
　　on how people are supposed
　　　　　　　　to live

If that's what
        you really feel
                wd please you
what in the world
            is stopping you from doing it?'"

On February 3
Ginsberg moved out of his hotel
(he'd broken with Sheila)
across the street from the Hotel Wentley
(famous from John Wieners' poem sequence)

and moved to 1010 Montgomery
Then 8 days later
            P.O. moved in also
He & Peter
        took vows to one another.
A.G. was reading many books
but writing little

He was interested in experimenting in W. C. Williams'
            triadic line
        or indented tercets
combined with Jack Kerouac's long-breathed lines--
when he turned 29 on June 3

Peter then went off to NY to visit his family.

Allen took a hitchhiking trip to Yosemite, Lake Tahoe, etc.
        then back to SF

One day in early August
He began typing
on a used typewriter
                on scratch paper
    with nothing to gain
            nothing to lose

the first 12 pages of "Howl"

        (He had a line from
        an earlier notebook

"I saw the best mind angel-headed hipster damned")

–I saw an early version of "Howl" at the
Whitney Beat show in '95
and remarked to Allen about the indentations
--which, of course, are not in the final version--
and he told me he had been
                imitating W. C. Williams–

Then, the same day he wrote those brilliant
long-breathed pages beginning with
"I saw the Best Minds of My Generation. . . ."

   he chant-jotted the Carl Solomon
              section (Part III)

Peter returned from his trip
              to the East Coast
When high on peyote
he & Peter went forth on a
peyote-halo walk in SF

and spotted
the Sir Francis Drake Hotel
looming in lit-up gloominess
        like the blood-eating fire god Moloch

So he added the
Part II Moloch section
        beginning "What sphinx of cement. . . ."

He began the revisions of Part I which
lasted a number of months

In September '55, A.G. and P.O.
moved to 1624 Milvia
        in Berkeley
           for $35 a month

revising revising revising revising
tuning the lyre for the Mind Entire.

# PART V

We left the story of the great Bard Allen Ginsberg
in the fall of 1955
when he was still revising "Howl"

## CITY LIGHTS

In 1953
a poet named Lawrence Ferlinghetti & Peter Martin
founded a paperback book store in San Francisco called
*City Lights Books*

A.G. and Ferl' met in August of '55
Ferlinghetti didn't want to publish *Empty Mirror*
but liked the manu of "Howl" Allen showed him--
and wanted to publish

## THE SIX GALLERY READING

Ginsberg learned that
a young bard from Wichita
Michael McClure
had been invited to set up a reading
at the Six Gallery
but had been too busy

Ginzap took over the planning
and lined up
McClure, Phil Whalen, Jack Kerouac, et al.
w/ Kenneth Rexroth as MC
for October 13, 1955
It was a Thursday

There were about a hundred
in the audience
First Philip Lamantia read
Then McClure's
"For the Death of 100 Whales"
then Phil Whalen
then an intermission

after which Ginsberg read "Howl" (Part I only)
building in confidence
                    --Kerouac shouting "Go! Go!"
          while beating rhythm on a wine jug--

The crowd was "blown away"
                    (to use the parlance of a few years later)

Ginsberg was in tears
                    by the time he roared to its end
as was Rexroth.

Snyder ended the Six Gallery reading
w/ his "A Berry Feast."

(A good account of the Six Gallery reading can be
found in Michael McClure's book *Scratching the
          Beat Surface*)

There was an actual orgy after the reading
which I always forgot
                    to ask A.G. to describe—
                    dang!

                    •

One afternoon
          on a SF bus
he came up w/
          the "Footnote to Howl" finale:
          the famous chant of "Holy Holy Holy . . ."

## 1956

Naomi died on June 9, 1956
                    while Allen was in California
As the casket was lowered
at Beth Moses Cemetery
                    in Farmingdale, LI
the rabbi would not chant Kaddish
because a minyan
                    (10 men)
                    was not on hand

*Naomi quiescat*

It ate at his heart
        she'd not had the proper chant
and he began a search
            to write one on his own.

In July of '56 Ginzap took off
on a ship, the USNS *St. Pendleton*
carrying Cold War stuff
        to the arctic circle
        for the Defense Early Warning
            radar apparatus up there

carrying the proofs of *Howl*
        which City Lights had set
(printed at Villiers Press in London)

There were errors in the line breaks of the 10-league lines
He had to pay for the fix-ups himself!
        (Though it only ultimately cost $20
        he volunteered to pay up to $200!)

While on ship, Phil Whalen forwarded mail
to A.G. (which he picked up in Takoma)

One was a letter from Naomi
just before she died

She mentioned the mimeographed "Howl" he had
sent her, and she lamented how
        "I still have the wire in my head."

        "I'm looking for a good time," she wrote
        "I hope you are not taking drugs
            as suggested by your poetry.
        That would hurt me.
            Don't go in for ridiculous things.
        With love and good news.
            Naomi"

After *Howl* was published in August '56
Ginsberg sent out oodles of copies

among the recipients:
Pound, Moore, Eliot, Auden, Jeffers, Charlie Chaplin,
Carl Solomon, Patchen, et numerous others
                                        over 100 copies

There was a big article in the
September 1956 *New York Times*
by Richard Eberhart
on "West Coast Rhythms" which ID'd A.G.
as an important  young poet.

A.G. always helped his friends
                    get their books published
This is not so common
                    among literati

It was the Best Minds factor
Ginsberg promoting his friends
Kerouac, Corso, Burroughs, Snyder, Whalen, & even
            Levertov, Niedecker, Oppenheimer, et al.

                    Fall o' '56
                    Ginsberg
                    met Denise Levertov
                    in Guadalajara
                    & added her
                    manuscript o' poems to
                    his collection
                    to show editors

            Returning to NYC the same fall
            Peter and Allen stayed with Elise Cowen
            in what is known as Yorkville, in Manhattan,
            Upper East part.

A.G. had manuscripts by Snyder, Whalen, Duncan, Dorn,
Creeley, Lamantia, Levertov, McClure, and Charles Olson
      even

He surged into *The New York Times* offices
                                on West 43rd
and requested a review of *Howl*

(Don't you wish you had the guts
to do that for YOUR book of verse?)

*Mademoiselle*, thanks to the 'Zap, published Levertov
and even some Burroughs.
He approached *Time*, *Life*, *Esquire*, *The Hudson
Review*, *Partisan Review*, *The Kenyon Review*,
*The New Yorker*, New Directions, et al.
            demanding ink for himself
            and the Best Minds group

**1957**

            Ginsberg
helped persuade Don Allen
to do the famous San Francisco Scene
issue of
*Evergreen Review* (#2)

(which I purchased at the University of Missouri bookstore that fall)

            Early '57  Kerouac, Allen, Peter, Gregory
            split for Tangiers and Paris
            (Ginsberg loaned Kerouac $225
            for the passage, which he had a lot of trouble
            getting repaid.)

            In Tangiers Allen spent 5 or 6
                        hours a day
                        typing Burroughs' manuscript
            later known as *Naked Lunch*
(Burroughs' concept of how even the reverse side print
            showing through as giving
            sense to text flow cut-up sequencing)

                        •

In March, U.S. customs seized 520 copies of *Howl*
            coming in from the printer in England

May 21
      two cops bought *Howl* at City Lights
                        and it was handcuff time

The American Civil Liberties Union took the case
with a trial scheduled for August 22

In October the judge declared "Howl" not obscene
a huge historic "victory" for a generation
        that had discovered new sounds for
        America's great Liberty Bell

The media hay harvested by Ginzap
from the "Howl" triumph
catapulted him into a worldwide fame
which was to last till his death
                in April of 1997
                almost 40 years later.

        In November 1957 Ginsberg wrote Kerouac
        from Paris
        announcing he'd written the lines
much of which later graced part IV of "Kaddish"

*Farewell*
*with long black shoe*
*Farewell*
*smoking corsets and ribs of steel*
*Farewell*
*communist party & broken stocking . . .*
*with your eyes of shock*
*with your eyes of lobotomy*
*with your eyes of stroke*
*with your eyes of divorce*
*with your eyes alone*
*with your eyes*
*with your eyes*
*with your death full of flowers*
*with your death of the golden windows of sunlight . . .*

# PART VI

We left the story of the great Bard Allen Ginsberg
in November o' '57
when he  wrote Kerouac
from Paris to announce he'd written many of the lines
that would later form one of the most riveting
        sections-- Part IV-- of his great poem "Kaddish"

He was already famous from the publication of "Howl"
and the victory by Lawrence Ferlinghetti's
City Lights Books
in the "Howl" obscenity trial.

## 1958

In February in London
he read all of "Howl"
felt full of tears
as the reading built in the
howlin' intensity he
gave those early readings
that he was reading to Blake himself
the "Soul in the Fog."

July '58, A.G. returned to NYC
He was a famous poet

and he had written some remarkable poems in Europe
"Death to Van Gogh's Ear"    "Poem Rocket"    "Europe! Europe!"
and the beautiful threnody "At Apollinaire's Grave"

He was more and more fascinated with Whitman's prophecy
of the Fall of America:

"I'd like to write a monstrous and golden political or historical poem
about the fall of America. . . .
talk about Dulles the way Blake talks
about the kings of France shuddering icy chill
runs down the arms to their sweating sceptres."

I remember how excited the NYC poetry scene was in 1965
when John Ashbery returned from living in Paris

It was the same whenever Allen returned
There was that klieg light buzz to a room
A hush and electric spark at his entrance

I think it was because he made you believe wherever he went
that the world was going to get better
through the power of Bardery alone

Jack Kerouac on the other hand
was having a bit of trouble with fame

Fame has a way of eating livers
and it was snacking away on the anxious author of *On the Road*

Kerouac's mom, Gabrielle, had been
sending hate letters to Ginsberg in Paris.

Meanwhile Ginsberg successfully urged James Laughlin
at New Directions
          to publish Corso and Snyder

                •

      We have already traced how when his mother died
      (Allen was in SF)
      the rabbi refused
      to chant the Kaddish
            because there was not a ten-man minyan
            to codify the chant

      His mind kept whispering "kaddish kaddish kaddish. . . "
      on his triumphal return to NYC
      after 18 months in Europe
            till one night in mid-November of 1958

      Allen was at the pad of a friend
      in the West Village named Zev Putterman
      They listened to Ray Charles
            Allen chanted from  Shelley's "Adonais"

      They took some morphine and meth
      in an pre-hep-B, pre-AIDS mode of needles and nickel bags

      He told the story of Naomi
      now dead three years
      and when he traced the tale of Naomi denied

            Zev Putterman found a copy and chanted it

      The 'Zap walked home from the West Side
      to his East 2nd Street pad after the Putterman Kaddish
      yearning 'pulsively
            to write

He jotted nonstop from 6 A.M. Saturday
                        till 10 P.M. on Sunday
            taking some Dexedrine
                        till 58 pages were done

He began editing and reworking in January '59
                        a process that lasted till '61.

## 1959

In early '59 a famous underground flick was filmed
                        by Robert Frank and Al Leslie
more or less based on Act Three of
Kerouac's play, *The Beat Generation*

The shooting lasted 6 weeks, but M-G-M had
            copyrighted the name B.G.
so it was renamed *Pull My Daisy*
                after the poem/tune written
                by Allen, Jack & Neal
                        back in '49

Also early that year a
benefit by Ginsberg at the Living Theater at 14th & 6th
(I attended)
            so that William Carlos Williams' *Many Loves*
                    could be produced

On February 5th a big reading at Columbia's McMillin
Theater
            1,400 packed the place
                    and 500 outside
--a kind of bardic vindication
for all his undergrad troubles.

It was around that time also
there was controversy over the banned issue
                        of the *Chicago Review*
A section of *Naked Lunch* was selected for publication
in the *Chicago Review* in early '59
plus Kerouac's "Old Angel Midnight,"
and prose by the estimable Edward Dahlberg

but a right-wing columnist in the *Chicago Daily News*
wrote about it in a column called
  "Filthy Writing on the Midway"

so that the university pulled it.

The 'Zap and Corso and Peter went to Chicago
to protest

(Allen read "Howl" in Chi
    which Fantasy released as a record)

There was a benefit for the *Chicago Review* legal expenses
at the Gaslight on MacDougal Street--
Miriam and I went
    We were students at NYU
      we'd met in Greek class
& on our dates
paid careful attention to Beat readings in coffeehouses
the Beat bookstores of 4th Avenue,
Beat folkies in the park, Beat summertime drum sessions
    on the Staten Island Ferry
    in honor of Edna St. Vincent Millay
& any place where poets clutched spring binders

(See the story "The Poetry Reading" in *Tales of Beatnik Glory*)

In the summer Ginzap went back to Cal.
& first took LSD as part of a research project
conducted by Gregory Bateson
at the Mental Research Institute in Palo Alto

While 'Zap was in Cal. that summer
Corso sold his TV, bed, etc.
    for cash to return to Europe.

## 1960

Allen kept polishing polishing polishing
the verse to be published in'61
in *Kaddish and Other Poems*

"I write so little,
            painfully & revise. . . I don't
have your football energy
                    for scrawling endlessly on pages. . . .
I guess all this publicity is bad," he wrote to Kerouac
after Kerouac had advised:
        "Beware of fame,
                poems will be nonsequitur"

                        •

Beat Political Split:

Kerouac supported Richard Nixon in the fall 1960 elections
Ginsberg Kennedy.

At Tim Leary's place on November 26, '60
he took some psilocybin
and believed he could cure
Leary's bad hearing
and fix his weak eyes

                Mr. Leary was hesitant
                to allow the naked Irwin Allen Ginsberg
                to roam the streets of Cambridge
                to preach love
                zonked in a pro tem Messiah mode

        **THE MAILER RULE:**
        (November 19, 1960)

        Do not stab your wife
        at the party
        where you
                are set to announce
        your candidacy for mayor.

At the same unfortunate party
Ginsberg and Norman Podhoretz
            --a famous Beatbaiter--
had a famous-at-the-time squabble
with Ginsberg calling P. a fuckhead
and P. calling G. an idiot.

# PART VII

And then came 1961
the year of the Kennedies

and Allen donated the handwritten draft of
"Kaddish" to the Living Theater
                           for a benefit
(De Kooning and Kline gave paintings
& Paul Goodman + John Cage also manu's)

Ginsberg was caught in the age-old
"You're famous, now what?" problem.

Allen took very seriously
his psychedelic experiences with Tim Leary

to the point he felt he had to proselytize
                           their use
           for a New Consciousness
           and a New Aeon

Among the first of those he turned on to psilocybin
were Thelonius Monk, Dizzy Gillespie, Willem de Kooning
Franz Kline & Robert Lowell.

"The Revolution has begun," he wrote to
Neal Cassady as a New Year's salute

           March 23, Peter and Allen departed for Paris
           on the SS *America*

           There was a young woman named Elise Cowen,
           who had typed the final version of "Kaddish" for Allen
           and very much in love with him

           She was there waving on the dock, with Allen's brother Eugene,
           Carl Solomon, Janine Vega, LeRoi Jones,
           and others

                      waving waving

In Paris 'Zap discovered
Burroughs had become obsessed with experiments in cut-ups
(a writing technique Brian Gysin had discovered)

> Burroughs used the cut-up method
> to break down what Burroughs called th'
> either/or "Aristotelian Construct"

Burroughs had checked out of the
Beat Hotel in Paris for Tangiers

& Corso, Allen, Peter Orlovsky
split to hang out at the Cannes Film Festival
                    then by boat to Tangiers
                    to hang with Burroughs

a crazy set of months
which scholars of Beatdom
                    nod and noodle over

Burroughs was always "difficult" as they say
and there were plenty of miniature storms
            among those attracted to the author of *Naked Lunch*

The reviews for *Kaddish and Other Poems*
were coming in
            and were not of the type such
            a great poem should command

Allen left Morocco in late August for Greece
He had royalties!  sacred royalties!
One check from Ferlinghetti for the
                    big sales of *Howl*

and another--$450--from the magazine *Show Business Illustrated*
for a piece on the Cannes Festival

After Greece, he went to Israel
where he met the socialist theologian Martin Buber

then
        the 'Zap
        was depressed going
        to India (first from Israel to Kenya)

some say because he seemed to have lost his
sense of identity.

Perhaps Burroughs' cut-up method, in part,
had pared away the power, word & image
& flung the Bard into a place
       of frantic futility & galactic mush-gush

He was singing the "Famous First Book/You're Famous/
What Next? Blues."

(I'd heard he was depressed--- I was a 22-year-old student
at New York University--
and began sending him issues of my mimeographed magazine
*Fuck You/ A Magazine of the Arts*
which, when he wrote back, he told me
had helped bring him out of his darkness

(part of his depression perhaps came after his
friend Elise Cowen-- in February of that year-- had
jumped from her parents' apartment window
              to her doom
--see Joyce Johnson's fine book *Minor Characters*
for more information on Elise Cowen,
whose poetry I published in my magazine.)

Allen's self-analysis
in India:
not to be so
      Jeremiah-like
& drive opponents
into a raging corner.

One of the greatest of nature poets, Gary Snyder,
and his brilliant wife Joanne Kyger
          arrived in Delhi in late February '62
          just days after Allen and Peter O

The four soon split for the Himalayan foothills
in search of a well-known holy man named Swami Shivananda

Ginsberg was to search and search
          in India for the final answers from holy guys

Snyder, of course, knew much about Zen practice
and in his calm teacherly way
      tried to fill the frenetic Allen
            in on the waves of Zen

They traveled more, and went to the town where the Dalai Lama
had set up his Tibetan gov't in exile

The Dalai Lama granted the four an hour's audience

He was not that interested in trying acid.

     It was in India, after many travels
     that the mail caught up with A.G.:
     the news that Elise had suffered a nervous breakdown
                    and jumped.

In Bombay, just before Joanne Kyger and Gary Snyder
were to leave the country

Gary, Allen and Peter
gave a public reading
      attended by over 100, including the American consul--

          Summer of '62
          Lawrence Ferlinghetti
            was reluctant
            to accept
            either one
            of A.G.'s
            suggested titles:
            *Bunch of Poems*
            or
            *Hiccup*
            for the tome teleos'd
            as
                *REALITY SANDWICHES*

# PART VIII

We left the story of the great bard Allen Ginsberg
when he was in India with his mate Peter Orlovsky
in 1962

His great books, *Howl and Other Poems*
                and *Kaddish and Other Poems*
had already been published

He was an international celebrity
yet he was in a depressed mood in India

and was seeking out holy men
          and learning the mantras & melodies
he was soon to bring to America
            and sing
with his ever-present finger cymbals--

The poets Gary Snyder and Joanne Kyger, then married,
joined Allen and Peter

They traveled to the Himalayan foothills to see
            Swami Shivananda
and then to visit the Dalai Lama
before Snyder and Kyger returned to their
            home in Kyoto, Japan.

In May '62 the 'Zap visited Sikkim where he met Gyalwa Karmapa

considered a direct descendant
of the Buddhist poet Milarepa
        who lived around 1000 A.D.

The meeting went well
    "He offered to
        teach me tantra
   & I offered to
        teach him pills,"
           he later humorously described it.

In the fall of '62 Ginsberg went
what I would call ghat-batty

He began to visit the Nimtallah Ghats in Calcutta
smoking pot (with many others there also)
  "a strange visionary experience"
  which helped him to observe the ghastliness
  with a measure of calm, as he jotted to Kerouac

watching the burning bodies
with fakirs & sadhus
  who sat in groups

& the mourners in white robes smoking ganja and singing hymns

with a circle of blind men, beggars,
    tum-tum-tumming on drums

bodies being oiled and placed on the pyres
roiling and rolling
  in the foreverness

Ginsberg went a number of times to these once-a-week ghat-fires

When he told me about it later
it seemed as if it was his first hands-on study of death
    and it was just the beginning

for no other poet in history
  not even Poe or Shakespeare
    studied death so intently.

  His ghat-visits coincided with
  the Cuban missile crisis
  when it REALLY SEEMED as
    if there might be a worldwide
      nuclear Boom-Boom.

  At the end of '62
  Peter and Allen split by boat
  Calcutta to Benares

There were many more adventures, such as visiting the Taj Mahal,
but it is the tale of how Allen Ginsberg aided
someone left for dead in the streets
                        that to me throws up a giant torch
                                    on his humanity


It was early 1963
Kennedy was still alive
The missile crisis had ebbed
and the Cold War seemed likely to decline
                        with a touch of grace from peace-minds


One day on a street where humans were left to die
Ginzap came across a guy in the fetal position
wasting away, flies eating the red meat of his wounds--
                    a soon and certain visitor to the worms.


There was a red teacup nearby

A.G. washed the cup and offered the gentleman some water
Then he brought him some curried potatoes
                        he was too weak at first to eat
Allen then went to the Ganges to wash his clothes
and when he returned the
            dying naked man still lay in the same spot
                            in the light of the sun
He asked a young man nearby what the naked man wanted
and the young man replied that he wanted to be
                        carried to
                            the water
Allen and Peter toted him to the river
                and washed him


In the coming weeks they tended to his care
Brought him a mattress
            hired a guy to wash and feed him


Allen finally learned he'd been tortured and had his tongue cut
out by Muslims
            and had a brother on the other side of India


Allen contacted the brother, and the brother came to Benares
Allen then demanded that a local hospital admit the man

and by the time the brother arrived
the wounded man
      was able to leave Benares with his brother by train--

      A classic Allen Ginsberg anecdote

•

He came away from India with
the concept of sacred singing

For instance when he had visited the Caves of Ajanta
with Gary Snyder

      he'd marveled at Snyder's singing
      of the *Prajnaparamita sutra*--

Allen then decided to chant mantras at his readings

(Allen made sure that all of his friends got
copies of the *Prajnaparamita sutra*
      Mine resides on the wall of my Woodstock studio)

He flew from Calcutta to Bangkok in May of '63
then to Saigon
      where the U.S. was just then beginning its
            twelve-year violence

Then to Cambodia to see the beauty of Angkor Wat
and wrote his well-known poem of the same name

then on June 11 to Japan
for additional time with Gary Snyder and Joanne Kyger
            in Kyoto

He was there for five weeks
then took a train to Tokyo
      On the train he wrote his eery, scary
          poem-chant "The Change"

in which he summarizes his spiritual quest
since the 1948 vision of William Blake

through all the spiritual flashes
of the 1950s and early '60s
the burning ghats of Calcutta
the visits to holy people

and, simply stated, decided
that it was time to renounce the impersonal concepts
of "Vision"
and return to the body.

He sent me the poem "The Change"
and I published it that year in my magazine
at a secret location in the Lower East Side.

# PART IX

We left our tracing
of the great bard A.G.
after he wrote a poem
important to his bardic path
called "The Change"
on the Kyoto-Tokyo express in July o' '63

in which he pulled away from his intense drive
for universal vision
and a Hunger for Prophecy & Futurity
and came to know the "truth of only the
body" as in the halls of the Kremlin
and Kennedy's dooméd White House

"the schemers draw back
weeping from their schemes."

On the hurtling iron horse he jotted,
"In my train seat I renounce
my power, so that I do
live I will die. . . ."

He was headed back to the USA
from travels to India, Japan and SE Asia
in '62 & '63

no longer needing to alter
the unalterable.

He had an invitation to a poetry conference in
Vancouver organized by Robert Creeley
in July of '63

It was a big success
and Ginzap was out of his doldrums.

The great Charles Olson
also at the Conference
told Allen, "I am one with my skin."

Allen was also
"I'm actually happy,"
he wrote his father

After Vancouver
Allen returned to San Francisco
staying with Lawrence Ferlinghetti and his wife, Kirby

Ginsberg then moved back into one of his old apartments in SF
on Gough
and his early love Neal Cassady and his girlfriend Anne Murphy
moved in also!

(Cassady had already met Ken Kesey
and the proto-Merry Pranksters
on their voyage into Learyland)

## THE BEGINNING OF THE VIETNAM WAR

Madame Nhu
sister-in-law of Pres. Diem of 'Nam
was coming to 'Frisco
and A.G. decided to join the protesters

He fashioned one of the most unique posters in
the history of peacework,

printing the following on a large sign
on which he also sketched the Buddha's footprint
three fish joined at one head:

**Name hypnosis and fear is the**
**Enemy—Satan go home!**
**I accept America and Red China**
**To the human race.**
**Madame Nhu and Mao-Tse Tung**
**Are in the same boat of meat.**

However interesting as a sign in a picket line
outside the Sheraton Palace Hotel

the Vietnam War was to continue
                              another 12 years.

### 1964

Late in '63, Allen flew back to NYC
experiencing a severe money drought

Robert Frank wanted to make a movie of "Kaddish"
so the bard went every other day
                    to Frank's house to write a possible scene

For each, Frank, the bard later wrote, paid him $10

"& thus kept me in money for about two months
while I was getting on my feet again."

Finally Allen gave it up, because
of the "areas of embarrassment & invasion of privacy"
as he jotted in his diary
if he had transformed elliptical verse
to the harsh light of dialogue.

In early '64
'Zap met Bob Dylan
at Ted Wilentz' house
          through the writer Al Aronowitz

Ted & Eli Wilentz had the very best bookstore on the set
It was then at 8th Street and MacDougal

and above it Ted lived
and had set up a kind of literary salon.

Thus began an association 'tween bard and minstrel
that lasted from '64
all the way to Ginsberg eagerly trying to stay alive
in early 1997, diagnosed with liver cancer,
in order for Dylan, Paul McCartney, Patti Smith,
et al

      to perform in an MTV salute to the 'Zap.

•

      It was now too that I met the bard
      and we began the first series of many capers
      together

The first was when he drew the cover stencils
for a little book by William Burroughs called
             *Roosevelt After Inauguration*

which I published in February '64
when the printer refused to allow it in
        the City Lights edition
          of *Yage Letters*

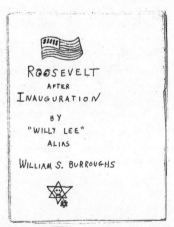

*Allen's Hand-drawn Cover for the Fuck You/ Press
edition of* Roosevelt After Inauguration

I felt so incredibly awed & honored
when he treated me
      as an equal

He took me to parties and introduced me to
literati such as Norman Podhoretz, John Hollander
                         & Mary Frank

Allen & Peter O moved to a legendary pad
at 704 East 5th
       in the Lower East Side

My Peace Eye Bookstore was just about to open
a few blocks away
           at 383 East 10th
& a few months later we began to hold rehearsals there
for a folk-rock poesy/satire band called The Fugs

Some of the ambience of A.G.'s place on East 5th
can be picked up in *Tales of Beatnik Glory*,
particularly the story
"Siobhan McKenna Group Grope"

         I was putting out "rare book" catalogs
         and had just graduated from NYU
         One day I went over to Ginzap's pad
                to scrounge some literary relics
                for my catalog
         I'd heard
         of a signed Dylan Thomas
                dress shirt
         that'd shown up in someone's catalog.

         A.G. graciously donated his cold-cream jar
         by the bed, and inscribed it as follows:

         "This is the jar of bona fide ass-wine or cock
         lubricant, into which I regularly plunged my
         hardened phallos to ease penetration of P. Orlovsky . . .
         winter 1964," and signed it.

         It was not the fastest-selling item
                in my catalogue
         &, as I recall, I gave it later
                to Richard Avedon
         during a Fugs photo shoot.

•

All of a sudden the real estate people were
calling the grid of tenement streets
(slums since after the War of 1812)
                    the East Village

and something called Underground Newspapers
                    were beginning to happen--
The *L.A. Free Press,*  the *Berkeley Barb,*
and *The East Village Other,*
          (the latter founded in '64 and named by the bard Ted Berrigan)

•

He tried to visit Kerouac,
who was living with his mother Gabrielle
                    in Northport, Long Island

Allen could be persistent
Once Allen waited by the bushes while Peter Orlovsky knocked
but Gabrielle refused to let O. in
          or, when Allen called,
                    to take any messages or #s

•

Even though it was Freedom Summer in Mississippi
          with Freedom Schools
                    and a huge voter registration drive
          1964 was the year New York City suffered
          one of its unfortunate periodic
                    bouts of Authoritarianism

                    (the control-fetishes of Mayor Giuliani
                    in the late 1990s had their roots in earlier eras)

          Back in '62 something called the New York Coffeehouse Law
          had been enacted

          in which if a restaurant wanted to have live entertainment
          it had to acquire a "coffeehouse license"

          which required submissions of blueprints, installation of
          sprinklers, more fire exits, kitchen flues--

installations overseen by the ultracorrupt NYC Building &
Fire Code Departments.

Many of us, including Allen G., myself, d. a. levy, Diane Wakoski,
David Henderson, Ishmael Reed, Marguerite Harris & many others
read poetry in East Village coffeehouses
especially at the Café Le Metro on 2nd Avenue

For some reason, the Dept. of Licenses began to
bust poetry readings, if you can believe it

Allen Ginsberg, Ellen Stewart of the Café La Mama, Joe Cino, myself,
Jackson MacLow and others began to protest--
(young firebrands Henry Stern and Ed Koch helped us)
          We started a campaign that ultimately led
          to the city gov't pulling back
                    and letting verse be heard without chop-bust.

                    But it wasn't easy, and it wasn't instant.

                    Then, late in 1964, LeMar
                    The Committee to Legalize Marijuana
                    was formed

(and there was a demonstration,
I think it was January 10, 1965
outside the Women's House of Detention
                              in the West Village
in a mild snow
with Allen, snowflakes on his beard,
                    holding a "Pot Is Fun" sign
one of the most widely spread images of the time.)

                              •

NYC in '64 also cracked down on Lenny Bruce
He had a way of putting together crisply timed and
                    brilliant routines that ruffled prudes
                              and angered squares--

His routine on Adolf Eichmann is as controversial now as it
was 33 years ago.  Ditto for his vignettes on Jacqueline Kennedy
and the JFK assassination & the one on Eleanor Roosevelt's bosom.

(Bruce's famous Rule #16 [deny deny deny, even if you're caught]
is being used right now, as I type this
during the Clinton/Lewinsky Spurtgate
                                    controversy)

Bruce was arrested in NYC
and Allen developed a petition in his defense
which was signed by a wide selection of Americans,
from young Woody Allen through Reinhold Niebuhr to Bob Dylan,
Lillian Hellman, Susan Sontag, Paul Newman, John Updike
                                              & many others

## PART X

The great bard Allen Ginsberg
was invited to Cuba
                by the minister of culture
to a writers' conference in Havana
in January o' '65

The state department said no,
but the bard threatened to sue
so he was given a visa

(Many of us would have muttered, "Oh, the
gummint doesn't want me to go, I'd better
                            change my plans,"
but not Ginzap)

The rules allowed him to fly in via Mexico City
but he had to RETURN by way of Prague

The CIA and its pals in organized crime
were desperate to snuff Fidel

and the political climate in Cuba
                        was on its guard

That's not all that was on its guard
for reasons that are utterly unobvious
America had its own worshiper of surveillance
                            & violation of privacy

one J. Edgar Hoover, then
>        the head of the FBI
>        and busy already

trying to disrupt the antiwar movement
and overestimating (it kept his budgets & prestige high)
the threat to the Flag from America's miniscule Communist Party

Anyway, J. Eddie Hoov'
>        that spring o' '65
sent out a one-page secret document
declaring Irwin Allen Ginsberg "potentially dangerous"

& possessed of a "propensity for violence and antipathy
>        toward good order and government":

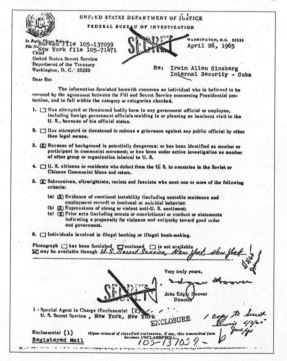

Things started out okay

He was given a spacious room at the Havana Riviera.

Ginsberg was ever attentive
            throughout his career
to the concept of having fun at night

so the first evening he took a bus to La Rampa
                        known for its nightlife

There he was approached by some young men
who published a literary magazine called *El Puente*
                                    *(The Bridge)*

        They asked if he was Allen Ginsberg
        Yes, he was

        and they took him to an out-of-the-way club
        and began to speak freely about the oppression in Cuba

        There was a police group, they said, called Lacra Social
                                which was harassing gays

        and those known derisively as *los infernos*
        –apparently a Cuban type of beatnik.

        People could be arrested for long hair and beards
        even though it was Castro's own appearance

    The young people asked Ginsberg to tell Castro about
    the persecution from Lacra Social

        As swamped with interviews and attention as anywhere else
        Allen began speaking in public against Lacra Social
                            and the accusations of oppression

A reporter asked Allen what he would encourage Castro
to do, should he get to meet him

Allen said he would inquire why Lacra Social was
abusing *los infernos*, and gays
and why pot was not legal, and why not do away
with capital punishment and instead give
those prisoners magic mushrooms and
jobs such as being the elevator operator
                        at the Havana Riviera hotel?

Allen kept bringing up the issues
in interviews

He visited Hemingway's house
and was a judge
at the festival's poetry competition

One of Allen's translators
was a young man
who had translated *Kaddish*

This young translator was taken to the
police station one night
and asked about his
association with the 'Zap

The man was detained again
after an evening in a theater
and Allen was angry

He demanded an explanation
from the Cuban minister of culture, Haydée Santamaria,
during a meeting he had with her.
Haydée Santamaria was a
heroine of the revolution & revered in Cuba–
She had watched her fiancé and her brother too
tortured to death by Batista's goons

Allen was upset at what she said,
that Cuba was taking a stand on homosexuality
because "too many gays
were making public spectacles
of themselves and seducing impressionable
young boys"

and, in a moment that caused a national scandal,
Ginsberg pat-swatted her rear
as she left the room.

Things grew chilly in Cuba right away
for the American bard
His poetry reading was canceled at the university

He learned that the minister of culture
was also upset with Ginsberg
                for suggesting that Raul Castro was gay
                and Ché Guevara cute
At a luncheon a few days later
Ginsberg tried to set things right
                with Haydée Santamaria
        on the rear-swat
        He'd meant it to be friendly
                        he said

She was in addition miffed over Ginsberg's
                talking about marijuana
                        to young people

Allen countered her upsetness
by suggesting that Cuba invite the Beatles
                (whose *Help!* was just out)
                        to perform

During the discussion on having the Beatles, Santamaria said
"They have no ideology
We are trying to build a revolution
                with ideology."

        Ginzap's days in Cuba
        were going into the toss-out countdown

After a couple of parties
        —'65 was a year in which
                there was often a party
                        AFTER the party
and so it was that night: back-to-backers,

and finally he was asleep around 6 A.M.
        when three soldiers
                & an immigration official
        beat on his door

        and took him to the airport
                to a plane bound for Czechoslovakia.

## THE KING OF THE MAY

In Prague, Allen was treated well
      He was a guest of the Writers' Union
      and was the beneficiary
      of one good aspect of a socialist country:
      there were performance royalties
      due him, built up in a bank
      from  his poetry being
           read by others at a literary café
      There were also other royalties
              from a book of his poetry
              published in Czech

There was the sense of thaw in Prague
         that three years later would lead to the
                 famous Prague Spring
      (followed by a Soviet invasion)

Allen was having a ball
He was always thrilled by the
         hundreds who wanted to interview him

& he was the hero in the neobeat café known
as the Viola
      where huge blow-ups of Fred McDarrah's
      photographs of American artists and Beats
      were arrayed on the wall

He wrote an excellent love poem
    "Message II"
        from Prague to Peter Orlovsky
        (p. 348 in *Collected Poems*)

Allen planned to stay a month in Prague
    including trips to Moscow and Poland.

In late March of '65 he trained from Prague to Moscow
        chrono-tracking himself in his intricate journals.
    His diaries always scorched with
         his erotic explorations on the road
      which, as we shall see,
          would betrouble him yet again
         with another authoritarian/police state

In Moscow the famous bard
             was the official guest of the Writers' Union
             once Tolstoy's mansion

Lots of smoked salmon, borscht, vodka, caviar and
             visits to St. Basil's, the Kremlin, the Pushkin
             Museum and the
             huge Gum dept. store
He met the poet Yevgeny Yevtushenko
     and true to his relentless vision
             Ginsberg plied him with his theories
             of open gayness, ganja and LSD

This was Russia after all, land of a million ears,
and Yevtushenko asked him not to continue
   "I feel rejected," A.G. said after the rebuff from
      Yev'.

Nor did Yev' dig Kerouac's theories about
             spontaneous composition.

With the poet Andrei Voznesensky however
         the bard formed a long term bond
             that lasted the rest of his life

Ginsberg went to Leningrad, toured the Hermitage
then went by train to Warsaw,
      where on April 10
         another one of his fine peripatetic works
         "Café in Warsaw" (page 350 of *Collected Poems*)

  then to Krakow, and by car to Auschwitz
         --there's a famous snapshot of A.G.
           by the *Arbeit Macht Frei*
             gates of the evilness zone

Then it was back to Prague
just in time for the ancient festival
         in honor of May Day
     called Majales

The commies had banned it about 20 years
and '65 was the first year
        it was reallowed

Students were to vote for a King of the May
and there would be a beauty pageant to
        select a Queen

By a strange series of circumstances
(the poet Josef Skvorecky was to have been the King
but he became ill)
Allen was voted in as the Kral Majales
        the King of the May!

He had always wanted to be the world's
        King of Maytime
so it was something
        that made him smile the rest of his life

On May 1 Allen was brought to the May Day parade
wearing a golden cardboard crown
        escorted by five beauteous damosels,
and a rout of students
        some with top hats and canes
        right out of the 1890s

He was dazzle-driven on a flatbed truck through Prague
        clinging his finger cymbals
        and singing mantras

thousands and thousands pouring to the streets
        driving past Franz Kafka's pad
        with Allen giving speeches
        like someone out on the stump
        whenever the truck should stop

Allen had been elected King of the May by
        an overwhelming vote
        and the partying continued till midnight
the moment the Queen was to be elected.

The Czech Communist Party secretary for cultural affairs

waxed furious at
>the spectacle of a gay beatnik
>>chanting to Shiva
>>>& eyeing guys

elected the Kral Majales

and so on the spot nullified A.G.'s election
>and called a halt to the nominations for Queen.

It was too late
>as evinced by the bard's fine poem
>>"Kral Majales," p. 353 in *Collected Poems*.

Meanwhile the secret police had placed A.G. under surveillance
'Zap was a secret policeperson's dream come true
They all drooled to surveil him
>J. Edgar Hoover
>the Cuban police
>and now the Czech

One of Allen's notebooks came into the possession
>of the Czechoslovakian fuzz

>I recall a few months later at the Berkeley Poetry Conference
>he described some of the items in the notebook
>>that might have put secret police in a tizzy
>>--one in particular
>>>that described erotic experimentations
>>>>with a broom

On May 5 he was punched and hit by a man
>snarling with homophobia—then
>taken in custody by police

>The officer snarled "Bouzerant!  Bouzerant!"
>>Fairy!  Fairy!

>Allen hummed the seed syllable "Om"
>>to quell the violence

Then he was set free, but next day

police said they had his notebook
and at the police station
they told him it was being turned
over to a prosecutor for illegal writings

And then he was tossed from another
                        authoritarian nation

        "due to many complaints about your presence
    in Prague from parents and scientists and
    educators who disapprove of your sexual
            theories."  This was May 7, the
            day he wrote the powerful

                        "Kral Majales"

He was held incommunicado
        and put on a flight to London
        where he was to hang out with
                Dylan
                    and the surging Beatles.

# PART XI

    Allen always loved the time
            he was the
            King of the May

    in a country where they had just
    begun to allow Kafka's *The Trial*
                        to be published
                        again–
    driven through the streets of Prague
    past Kafka's house
    clink-clanging his
                finger cymbals
    and wearing a golden crown

    It had been one of those
                    frozen moments of fun

Then the police had come for him

and shipped him to London
        They'd stolen one of his notebooks
        & he was upset about it

On the plane he wrote his poem

              "Kral Majales"

## GINSBERG MEETS THE BEATLES

There was some genius-level music
being made in '65
by the Beatles
        and Bob Dylan

Both the Beatles & Dylan were in London
when the kicked-out Kral Majales from Kafkatown
                        arrived.

Dylan was in the middle of making his movie
              *Don't Look Back*
and the Beatles were on their prophet-train roll
        preparing the soundtrack album of *Help!*
        (In a few weeks, for instance,
                they'd record their great tune "Yesterday")
Ginsberg went to Dylan's concert at Royal Albert Hall
There was a party afterwards
& Ginsberg was invited to the suite
where Dylan and the Beatles were gathered.

D. and the Beatles had met already
the previous year
but, for some reason, there was considerable silent tension
at this meeting of the essence
        of the Rhymed Song Folk/Pop Complex &
Ginsberg tried to "break the ice" as they say

He fell into Lennon's lap and asked if he'd ever read Blake
Lennon had once edited a magazine at art school
              called the *Daily Howl*

and a bit of ice was dislodged
        on the shores of fame.

(Ginsberg began a friendship with Paul,
        and later with Linda McCartney
that lasted the rest of his life
There was a big oil painting by McC. in the guest bedroom of
                Ginsberg's loft)

Next day the bard went to the embassy
        to try to get his notebook back from the
                Prague police

There was a party for Ginzap's 39th birthday
        at a London bookstore
–rock & roll, miniskirts, Tom Jones shirts, & lots of see-through–

John & Cynthia Lennon
        plus George Harrison & Patti Boyd
            came to th' bard's party

    Allen was a bit drunk
    as he rushed to greet
        the ill-at-ease singers
    (who were glancing around to make sure
            no cameras were snapping)
    for the 'Zap was naked,  wearing his jockey shorts on his head,
    and a "Do Not Disturb" hotel doorknob sign
             attached to his Clinton.

            •

Allen spent time with the poet Basil Bunting in Newcastle
Bunting had been a pal of Pound and W. C. Williams
and had been "rediscovered"
        by young English poets

Ginsberg's June '65 poem "Studying the Signs" after reading
        Bunting's book *Briggflatts*.

Another distilling beautiful 4-page poem,
        from the chaos of the first half
    of '65, "Who Be Kind To"' p. 359 in the
            *Collected Poems*

was written for the International Poetry Reading
        at Royal Albert Hall on June 8

(which Allen and the filmmaker Barbara Rubin
                              organized--
with 7,000 people in attendance,
                        including Indira Gandhi)

Then a week in Paris
strip-searched at JFK and a pocket-lint search
                              for pot

returning to the USA  June 29.

## HALL DANCE OF GUGG JOY

Most of us who are honored
with Guggenheim Fellowships in verse
wait patiently
          for the check
but not A.G.
          who, upon returning to the States,
raced to the Guggenheim offices
on Park Avenue South

to do a dance of Nike! Victory! Triumph!
                              and Joy of Cash!
through the hallways and offices
(and perhaps also to get
            the fellowship check
            a little ahead of schedule)
The Guggenheim gave him the largesse
for one of his most important poetic ventures–
He purchased a VW camper
            & outfitted it with a desk, bed & icebox

so that he could drive around the nation
          while composing a series of travel poems
              including the fine "Wichita Vortex Sutra" of '66

                        •

In July Allen flew to SF
              for the Berkeley Poetry Conference
one of those gatherings
          whose impact ripples out through
          decades in the world of
                    poesy & theory–

Gary Snyder, Robert Creeley,
Jack Spicer (who would pass away soon after), Robert Duncan
John Wieners, the great Charles Olson
plus some of us (then) younger bards:
Ted Berrigan, Lenore Kandel, and myself

(Donald Allen, editor of the *New American Poetry* anthology,
arranged for Grove Press to fly me out
        --many thanks to Grove Press, which I too casually
        forgot formally to thank 35 years ago)

Ginsberg read to a huge crowd in Wheeler Auditorium
where, later in the week, Charles Olson
        gave a genius-level Bacchic talk
            that astounded a generation.

In August, after the Berkeley Poetry Conference
A.G. went camping with Gary Snyder for a month
        in the Cascades, Crater Lake National Park,
        and Mount Rainier in Washington

      They were alone in the vastness
      reading Milarepa's poems aloud in the morning
          Allen learning again
          the ineffable Zen centerédness

        that made the bard Snyder
        such an emblem of the times.

## PART XII

        1965 was a great year
      to understand the soul of the great bard
             Allen Ginsberg
for it was then
we see how he refused to be isolated
          from the broader culture
no matter how controversial he might have seemed

and he dared to be his own history.

We have noted how

in August of 1965, after the Berkeley Poetry Conference
A.G. went camping with Gary Snyder for a month
                        in the Cascades, Crater Lake National Park,
                        and Mt Rainier in Washington

            alone in the vastness
            reading Milarepa's poems aloud in the morning

While Allen was away
I was picking up his mail for him in New York City—
My Peace Eye Bookstore was thriving on East 10th
and the Fugs were performing at standing-room-only
                        midnight concerts at the Bridge Theater
                        on St. Mark's Place

That August, while Ginsberg was in the mountains with Snyder
we learned of an attempt by the Federal Bureau of Narcotics
                        & Dangerous Drugs
                        (forerunner of the DEA)
to set the 'Zap up for a pot bust

            It was an archetypal event
            Allen responded to it
                        with his own investigation
                        conducted over decades

            into the involvement of U.S. gov't agencies
            in dealing and drug smuggling.

What happened was this:

A couple of young men,  Jack Martin & Dale Wilbourne
had been arrested for alleged
                        possession of marijuana

Four BNDD agents
        met with Martin
and threatened additional charges
        plus a bail bump-up from $5k to $100k
unless he set up Ginsberg
                for a pot arrest.

(Ginsberg had been very outspoken for legalization

The photo of him at a Lemar march
      with a "Pot Is Fun" sign
           had been published around the world)

"We want Ginsberg," one of the agents had said.

We learned about the incident
      & I put out a press release about it
The Fugs and others held a benefit for the defendants
      where the Federal agents in question
         showed up outside the gig
            and harassed people!

As a further emblem of his soul
      Ginzap did not quail
         and vacuum his pockets

Instead he went on the offensive
began clipping articles on
         how many times the police
themselves were arrested for selling drugs
started asking questions
      (Ginsberg I think asked more questions
      in his life
         than anyone in the history of
            Western Civilization)
and later, of course, the famous
         bet Ginsberg made with the
         head of the CIA, Richard Helms,
         over CIA involvement in the heroin racket

•

That fall, Ginsberg was in California
      & took part in large antiwar rallies
         in Berkeley & Oakland

organized in good part by Jerry Rubin.

(The Fugs drove across
      America in a VW van
         to take part in the rallies
One of our concerts

was with Ginsberg and Country Joe & the Fish
                              at UC Berkeley.)

There was a march from Berkeley
                    through the black area of Oakland
                and into downtown Oakland

Ginzap and Gary Snyder
                sang mantras
                          from a sound truck
to spread peace

But the police stopped the march
                      at  the Oakland city limits
& members of the Hells Angels bike gang
                      tore into the head of the march
                      and pulled down a
                      PEACE IN VIETNAM sign

They cut the speaker wires
            & the march ended right there.

Several weeks later
            another march was scheduled
            and the H. Angels again threatened violence

Allen organized a public forum
                    for a kind of debate 'tween
the Vietnam Day Committee
            (sponsor of the upcoming march)
and the H.A.'s.

The bikers came away
            still planning to disrupt the walk.

Then Ken Kesey
            proposed a meeting
                      'tween the march organizers & the bikers
at Sonny Barger's house in Oakland

The Angels had some kind of ultra-'noidal vision
of the Domino Theory
The D.T. held that, like a line of dominos falling in a flowing ripple

the nations of SE Asia would
                    tumble to commie

& it was somehow felt that
          the dominos led across the moily pacific
                              and would implode
                              upon a commie Oakland
--too much amphetamine.

Most of those at Kesey's pad
                    dropped acid
except Ginzap,
          who feared what they called in those days a
                                        Galactic Bummer.

The talk oozed acrimonious
till A.G. opened his small harmonium
              and began to chant the *Prajnaparamita sutra*

Soon some Angels joined the chant
and Neal Cassady, Ken Kesey
            and everybody finally.

Barger put Dylan's "Gates of Eden" on the player
and the Angels agreed not to
                    break up the rally

Allen wrote one of his better poems of the year,
"First Party at Ken Kesey's with
                    Hells Angels"
                    dated December '65.

It was an example of quality peacemaking
The Angels issued a press release
          they were not about to attack a bunch
                              of dirty commies

& the march occurred without any violence.

## PART XIII

We left off our tale of the great bard Allen Ginsberg
in the fall of 1965
when he intervened
                with the Hells Angels
to get them not to
                attack an antiwar march
                                in Oakland


Bob Dylan was in California in late '65
He gave Allen $600
                with which he purchased a
                reel-to-reel Uher tape recorder
                just about the finest you
                                could get in that era

(Dylan also bought the bard Michael McClure
an autoharp, and Peter Orlovsky an amplifier)

Allen took the Uher with him
It was portable, with a shoulder strap
                                and a handheld microphone
                                with a pause button

Thus, on the beach
                on the road
                        in the woods
                                at a party
                                        or at Ferlinghetti's cabin in Big Sur

Ginsberg could experiment
with a kind of spontaneous verse
                acutely observational in the mode of W. C. Williams
                with the long lines of Blake
                                & the eye of a photographer
                                        (Ginsberg's photos later became
                                        very well respected– he took
                                        literally tens of thousands of them,
                                        beginning in the 1940 proto-Beat-era
                                        all the way to his death in 1997)

Allen did his best work
        after periods of introspection & study
and now he was ready to take on a Whitman-level
study of America
            in early 1966
                with the Vietnam War
                throbbing in the background.

The war the war the war
Dylan's politics had shifted to the right
        as far as Vietnam was concerned
It chilled McClure when Dylan
            let it out &
refused to take a stand against
            the Vietnam War
and in fact took what would have been called
in the era
        an imperialist stance.

During recent months
Allen & his father, Louis,
had been arguing furiously by letter
           over the war

and it was in the context
of Blake, Uher, Williams,
        the beauty & balefulness of his nation
that Ginsberg
        began, in a few weeks,
        his great poem "Wichita Vortex Sutra"

## 1966

Tim Leary was arrested on 12-23-65
in Laredo for grass
On trial on 3-9-66
        and given thirty years in the slams!

My Peace Eye Bookstore was raided on January 1, 1966
& I was charged with obscenity
           for my magazine
      (though I later won the case)
Allen immediately did a benefit for me in Los Angeles

On January 26
the 'Zap began a long journey in his
new VW van
          across the USA
driven by Peter Orlovsky
                    and recording instant verse
                    in the front seat with his Uher

the line breaks
          indicated by the clicking
                    of the on/off switch

The camper meandered here & there in the west
and into Texas
          and then up to Kansas
          where the radio blurt-blared
                    with religiosity & war news

Barry Farrell, one of *Life* magazine's best writers,
traveled with Allen
                    on the Wichita Vortex trip
writing a big story, "Guru Comes to Kansas"

Driving in to Wichita
the bard began dictating the lines
that were to become the 18-page poem
                    which he finished on February 14.

"Thy sins are forgiven, Wichita!
                    Thy lonesomeness annulled, O Kansas dear!
                              as the western Twang prophesied
          thru banjo, when lone cowboy walked the railroad track
                              past an empty station toward the sun
                    sinking giant-bulbed orange down the box canyon–
          Music strung over his back
                              and empty handed     singing on this planet earth
                              I'm a lonely Dog, O Mother!
          Come, Nebraska, sing & dance with me–
          Come lovers of Lincoln and Omaha,
                    hear my soft voice at last . . ."

A post-acid post-Whitman song of a great nation.

published in *The Village Voice*
                        on April 28
                a further revelation
                        of his stature
                        as an American bard

•

Allen found time to write the liner notes
for the second Fugs record
                        which we recorded that spring.

•

April 17, Gordon Liddy, later
                        sent to jail for his role
                                in Nixon's dirty tricks team,
led a raid by Dutchess County police
on Tim Leary's huge 2,500-acre estate in Millbrook
                loaned to him by Billy Hitchcock

29 people were there and searched,
                and all 64 rooms of the mansion searched
but no grass was found.

Liddy was sure he had found something
                        ascribable to Leary
                                but it turned out to be peat moss

Allen helped organize a full-page ad in *The New York Times*
to help Mr. Leary

                In June Allen testified in D.C.
                against making LSD illegal
                        to no avail.

                The summer of '66
                saw the death of the brilliant poet Frank O'Hara
                struck down by a dune taxi
                        on Fire Island July 24

Allen wrote his
                "City Midnight Junk Strains"  for Frank O'Hara
                        (p. 457, *Collected Poems*)

The next day
Bob Dylan had his motorcycle accident in Bearsville
                an injured neck and other bruisings

        Three weeks later Allen visited Dylan
        bringing him some books, Rimbaud, Blake,
                        Dickinson, Shelley.

The fall of '66
        loomed like the frenetic highway
                        of the same name
hundreds of interviews, readings, letters, journal entries,
skin-slurps, hookahs, plane trips, arguments & kisses

He wrote "A Vow" on October 11
a fine example of what could be called the Scold Poem.
Like the great Norman Thomas,
the bard was sometimes content merely to scold--
singing his vision of calming down the Greed Machine
                (p. 460, *Collected Poems*)

Then came the great year of Flower Power, 1967

# PART XIV

## THE YEAR OF FLOWERS

Gary Snyder
began the Human Be-In
                on January 14
                in the Golden Gate Park polo field

    with a riff on a conch shell

The formal name for the event was
"Gathering of the Tribes for a Human Be-In"

The name of course
                came from the Sit-Ins
                        in the South
                        to integrate lunch counters, say,
                                at Woolworth's
    & later the popular Teach-ins
    against the war in Vietnam

Now it was Be-In
and this one event set the
                    cultural tone of the year
along with the rhymed doublet: Flower Power

There were 20,000 there to surge
                    in primary-color splendor
                    with the fine Pacific psyche-light
                    at last outshining
                            the Puritanical searchlight
                                    from Plymouth Rock

    as the Grateful Dead, Jefferson Airplane, Quicksilver
    Messenger Service, Jerry Rubin, Gary Snyder, Tim Leary,
    Lenore Kandel, Ginsberg & others
                        made words and music.

All across America that spring
there were Be-ins, Smoke-ins, Love-ins,
                    Tipi-ins and In-ins

Ginsberg was everywhere,
                    like a bardic blur
                            chanting his nation

& cling-clinging his finger cymbals.

        On
        February 12, for instance, a huge celebration in
        Toronto called "Perception '67"
                    with Marshall McLuhan, The Fugs, Paul Krassner

In May in Cleveland, a benefit for the ultraharassed young
                            poet named d. a. levy
                            one of America's
                                    great unsung.

                    ●

Ken Kesey had purchased a farm near Eugene, Ore
& 'Zap visited
        –Neal Cassady and the Merry Pranksters were there

May 25, they took the great psychedelic tour bus
                            called Further

on the road
> to a gig at Western State College in Oregon
> with the Jefferson Airplane

> It was the last time Ginzap would
>> see great pal Neal Cassady.

## JUNE 27

The year before
> after a Fugs concert
the police had invaded Peace Eye Bookstore
& seized many issues of
> *Fuck You/ A Magazine of the Arts*

I was arrested; the ACLU took my case
and after a trial before 3 New York judges
I was found not guilty

So I threw a victory party at Peace Eye June 27
>> 1967

The great bard was there
The place was totally packed
> on a hot summer night
when some neighborhood kids
> began to toss firecrackers
>> through the open door

> We went outside to cool them out
> A.G. came too

One of them was brandishing
> a wide-tipped hunting arrow
It was an emblem of Allen
as he sank to his knees on the sidewalk
>> in front of the wide-eyed youth
and made his hands in the shape of a mudra

The young man raised his arm back
> as if to hurl it into the bard's neck

but Allen's calm words
> caused him to put it down
>> to his side

–another emblem of conduct by a great poet

●

On July 5 'Zap flew to Italy
        for the Spoleto Festival, where he met Ezra Pound
        and tried to get Lb to abandon his famous multi-year silence
                though all he would do was shake Allen's hand
then it was off to London
& a party for 'Zap at James McNeill Whistler's house
Allen was always thrilled when the bacchants of rock & roll
                allowed him to hang with them
as when he sat in the recording booth
during the Rolling Stones' recording of "We Love You"
                        with Lennon and McCartney doing harmony

July 20
Allen gave a talk "Consciousness and Practical Action"
        at the Dialectics of Liberation Conference in London

at which, also, Gregory Bateson gave a seminar
        "Ecological Destruction by Technology"
        which astounded the American bard–
        Bateson had predicted Global Warming decades
                before it came to public parlance.

Allen took his father Louis and stepmother Edith
on what they call a "whirlwind" tour of Europe, then
after his parents had returned to the States,

July 28  driving to Wales
he stopped for a visit to Wordsworth's Tintern Abbey ruins
& then once in Wales
                a poem writ on acid, one of his better,
                called "Wales Visitation"

                        ●

That summer, while Allen was in Europe
his mate Peter Orlovsky was in Bellevue
                after too much amphetamine

        Peter was spotted in those months cleaning
        the cobbles of Avenue C with a toothbrush

I remember he sold me his Bellevue pajamas
for $6 one day in the park after he escaped
                    I wanted to wear them at Fugs shows

•

On September 23 drove to Sant Ambrogio to have lunch with
                    Olga Rudge & Ezra Pound

He brought along his harmonium
                    sang Lb the *Prajnaparamita sutra*–
          a few weeks later, in mid-October
          he visited Pound again at his winter home in Venice
          played "Eleanor Rigby" and "Yellow Submarine"
and Dylan's
"Gates of Eden" & "Sad-Eyed Lady of the Lowlands"

One evening he spoke at length with Pound
          after walking around Venice checking out
                    locations mentioned in *The Cantos*

Pound spoke finally of himself & his troubles–
"But the worst mistake I made was the stupid suburban prejudice of anti-
  Semitism.  All along, that spoiled everything."

                    October 21 was the day of the
                    Exorcism of the Pentagon in D.C.
                    & Allen visited again with Pound
                    & his longtime companion Olga Rudge

                    helping the grand old man of meter
                                        try to escape his past

                              *

                    Ginsberg was one of the greatest
                    givers in the History of Verse

Charles Rothschild, one of the managers of The Fugs,
began to help Allen get properly paid for his readings
Allen wanted
          what other famous writers obtained
          for barding
He'd formed a nonprofit corporation
                    the Committee on Poetry
                    (I was vice president for a few years)

to create a sense of order
      in the thousands upon thousands upon thousands
            that Ginzap gave away to help others.
In '67, the Year of Love
      he gave away around $20k

$4,000 to the filmmaker Jack Smith, $1,500 each to
      beat bro's Corso and Huncke
the West Coast communard Irwin Rosenthal, $2,500

$1,500 to the great artist/scholar/filmmaker Harry Smith
$400 to Ken Kesey, and money to the filmmaker Barbara Rubin,
to the bards Ray Bremser, Diane Di Prima, Amiri Baraka,
Charles Plymell, et alia bardifica

He paid the Chelsea Hotel bill for the English poet Basil Bunting
      when Bunting came to NYC
            to read at the Gugg.

He bought a new harmonium for Bhaktivedanta
      & four Vedic chanting records for Ezra Pound

       •

      Not all were so friendly
      The Diggers called a meeting that fall
            at the Glide Church in SF
on the question of money

      Digger Emmett Grogan had a penchant for shriek-fit
            and plied it then.

      The Diggers, he said,
      wanted "all the bands, stores, and people in this whole
            fucking hippie scene–go nonprofit. That means
            if you're a store you take that money you make
            & share it with the people who make
                your beads and sandals."

      Ginsberg was in the room, and suggested people
      turn themselves into foundations as he had done
            in forming the Committee on Poetry

Then he spoke directly to Grogan:

"What does a guy like me do who's making some bread
and decides he wants to buy a little piece of land?
I just bought some groovy Committee on Poetry land
          [He'd purchased some land in Nevada City, California
          with Gary Snyder and Richard Baker]

and like now I think I'd like
a little of something for myself.
*Just* for myself."

Grogan yelled back, "Let's cut the money
                    Say I make beads & you make sandals
                    we'll *trade* them

Ginzap: "What do you want me to do, carry my poems around
                                        and trade them?"

                    •

That fall, the murder of Che in Bolivia
& Allen's fine poem in response
"Elegy Che Guevara"   (Venice, November '67
                    p. 484, *Collected Poems*)

beginning with the startling image
               shown to the world
                    of Guevara's face in death
                              almost seeming to smile.

"One radiant face driven mad with a rifle"
                         he wrote
          "Confronting the electric networks"

## PART XV

The great bard Allen Ginsberg
kept his famous shoulder to the wheel
                    in  the ghastly year known as '68

In February
          Ferlinghetti replied

he loved Allen's next book of verse
*Planet News*
especially the beautiful poem from '67
called "Wales Visitation"


February was also the month
his friend and onetime lover Neal Cassady passed away
Cassady had gone to a wedding in
San Miguel de Allende
He'd left his bag at a railroad station
a few miles away
and after the party
drunk and high
he died on the tracks
walking back


He was the first of the beatnik hexad
to pass.
His "Elegy for Neal Cassady"
laid down beautifully the grief
of someone who'd lost a soul buddy
with memories of discourse
Spirit to Spirit
as in the lines,
"I could talk to you forever,
The pleasure inexhaustible
discourse of spirit to spirit,
O Spirit"
(p. 488, *Collected Poems*)


•


Late in February Allen (and the Fugs) performed
in Appleton, Wisconsin
where Senator Joseph McCarthy is buried

We performed an exorcism
that enraged the right.
Right-wing radio man Paul Harvey
growled enormously about it
on his show

but we summoned his soul
       --the Fugs, Ginzap, and about 50 locals--

with Allen commenting on the Great Redbaiter's homophobia
but we were respectful

Allen recited a Hebrew prayer, and an invocation to Shiva
and we recited the *Prajnaparamita sutra*
then sang "My Country 'Tis of Thee"

then a few minutes of Hare Krishna
       after which I chanted the final words of
       Plato's *Republic*
       in Greek

       people left friendly items
              on and around the stone

       then we got the hell out of there

## THE FARM

Huge stacks of mail
       and the endless ring ring of the phone

helped make the bard want to get to silence

& he asked filmmaker Barbara Rubin
             to look for a place in the country.

A big factor in wanting a country place
was to help get Peter Orlovsky off methedrine
       His condition had gotten more serious than
       toothbrushing the cobbles of Avenue C
           in a meth-addled thirst for cleanliness.

Peter, of course, was a poet of stature.  I often think of
his graceful lines in Don Allen's *New American Poetry:*
              ". . . on a hill a butterfly
makes a cup that I drink from, walking over a bridge
of flowers."

Allen and Barbara Rubin had been occasional lovers
He made it with women more often
                              than commonly known
& she apparently had a passion to marry the bard
a passion she shared with but a few of her friends

She looked around Sharon Springs and Cherry Valley
west of Albany,
              near Jewish summer resorts
She was increasingly drawn to orthodox Judaism
                    which may have led her where to search

She found an old farm outside Cherry Valley
surrounded by state forest
                    90 acres, run-down, no electricity

         Allen bought it
         & he and Barbara went to the farm mid-March '68

In addition to helping Peter,
who came to the farm with his oft-hospitalized brother Julius
Ginsberg also had in mind getting Kerouac up there
                          to dry out his liver
Though Barbara Rubin soon drifted away from her dreams
                          of marriage with the bard
the farm remained a factor, a haven for poets & seekers
for the rest of A.G.'s life
                    through the 1990s


### MAY 1968

         one of his more
controversial poems
              "Please Master"
         the 1st bardic evidence
         of his interest in what they call
                          "rough trade"

•

Allen agreed to come to Chicago in August
as part of a Festival of Life

It was intended to be a rock & roll antiwar peace party

but the year had other intentions
It was a year of pings
        –the pings of bullets

Martin King in April-- ping!
Robert Kennedy in June– ping! ping!

The great uprisings of students in Paris
                and at Columbia University
& the biggest antiwar movement
                        since just before World War I

So that by the time of the Chicago Democratic Convention
there were soldiers everywhere
                and a thuglike convention
                    where dissent was suppressed, as we shall see.
                    •

Allen had taught many of us the mantrams
he had brought back with him from India

and just before the Democratic Convention
he and I issued a statement
published in the underground press
calling for those who came to Chicago
                to chant OM
                        to quell the violence.

## GINSBERG IN CHICAGO, AUGUST 1968

Allen had an assignment (and press pass)
to cover the convention for *Esquire* magazine
(along with Terry Southern, William Burroughs and
Jean Genet, who sneaked in to Chicago from Montreal)

Allen's French was very good
        and I was amazed how well
        he translated for Genet

The city had refused to issue permits
for participants in the Festival of Life
to camp out in Lincoln Park

where each night at 11 P.M., the police
would billy-club and teargas everyone out of the park

Allen sang OM for hours,
>  and sometimes I joined in

## MONDAY, AUGUST 26

Barricades were built in Lincoln Park
>  to defend the right to sleep there
at 12:30 A.M. the police
>  clubbed and attacked the barricades

Tonight they marched behind
>  a street sweeper truck whose
>  water tanks had been
>  converted to hold tear gas!

(These ghastly police state devices
maybe gifts from Garden Plot or the CIA Chaos program?)

To me this was the last mote of proof
>  in 1968
>  that the Nation was lost

Ginsberg said
"I got gassed chanting AUM
>  with a hundred youthful voices
>  under the trees . . .

The Daily Mayor has written a
bloody vulgar script for American Children."

## GINSBERG SHOWS ABILITY AS
## HALFBACK DURING TEARGAS ATTACK

We left the park to return to the Hotel Lincoln
>  (next to Lincoln Park, where we were staying)
but there were snout-nozzled cops there
>  lobbing tear-gas grenades
which plomfed near our feet.
We crouched down and dashed through
>  the hostile molecules
heads low, knees high
>  as if we were halfbacks
>  on a high school football team
>  toward the lobby.

## TUESDAY AUGUST 27

At dawn on the 27th
                    Ginsberg came back  to the park
singing various mantras
                    for several hours
till his voice became hoarse and whispery.


Allen was the only bard in the history of Western Civilization
            to have over-ommed,
                that is, he'd uttered the seed syllable "Om" so many hours
                        trying to quell the violence
                                he peace-pained his voice
                                and was omming, at the end,
                                        like Froggie the Gremlin.


                    That night the protesters threw a
                    60th Unbirthday Party for Lyndon Johnson
                                at the packed Chicago Coliseum
            6,000 people were there
            While Phil Ochs sang "I Ain't Marchin' Anymore"
            a guy burned his draft card
            and then in one amazing sequence of seconds
            there was a sudden poof-up of
                                maybe a hundred blazing draft cards
                    pointillisticly patterning
                                the Coliseum audience.


            Ginsberg's voice had not yet returned
                        from his many hours
                        of chanting
                                    to quell the violence
            so he passed me a note to read
                        to the audience:


    "Introduce me as Prague King of May -- Ed-- in my turn,
you explain I lost my voice chanting Aum in park -- so please
you read my piece -- then I'll do 3 Minutes of Silence Mind
            consciousness & belly breathing"

## WEDNESDAY AUGUST 28

That afternoon
Daley had allowed
a single rally at the bandshell
in Grant Park
sponsored by the Mobilization--
From 10 to 15,000 showed up

About 4:30
Dave Dellinger addressed the crowd
through a portable bullhorn
to announce a nonviolent march to the Democratic Convention
4 1/2 miles
from Grant Park

Grant Park is connected to downtown via a series of bridges
across railroad tracks to the west
Lines of soldiers prevented the  march from leaving
over any of the bridges
and many of us sat down in front of the troops while
U.S. Army helicopters circled overhead

It was very scary
There were fixed bayonets
& jeeps with barbed wire
hippie-sweeping screens
plus the whoppa whoppa
of helicopters
that mixed with the songs  Phil Ochs
sang to calm us:

"We're the cops of the world, boys,
We're the cops of the world . . ."
& then his song
"Outside of a Small Circle of Friends"
singing through the bullhorn
someone was holding to his face.

Then Allen Ginsberg,
still hoarse from singing seed syllables
in the rings of violence
chanted "The Grey Monk" of William Blake
through the bullhorn

All of us who were sitting and waiting
were chatty and restless
yet by the time he chanted (from memory)
              the final verses of the wounded Grey Monk
      All grew silent
              except the ghastly helicopters:

"Thy Father drew his sword in the North,
With his thousands strong he marched forth;
Thy Brother has arm'd himself in Steel
To avenge the wrongs thy Children feel.

But vain the Sword & vain the Bow,
They never can work War's overthrow.
The Hermit's Prayer & the Widow's tear
Alone can free the World from fear.

For a Tear is an Intellectual Thing,
And a Sigh is the Sword of an Angel King,
And the bitter groan of the Martyr's woe
Is an Arrow from the Almightie's Bow.

The hand of Vengeance found the Bed
To which the Purple Tyrant Fled;
The iron hand crush'd the Tyrant's head
And became a Tyrant in his stead."

        A few of us had pushed fresh daisies
into the rifle barrels at the Pentagon
        just 10 months ago
        and now, even though
              I again had fresh white flowers
      I knew this was a different type of event
            and that I would likely have been
                    bayoneted and shot
              pushing petal in metal

Finally, after hours of negotiations,
the protesters found a way
        of getting out of Grant Park
and they surged
      across a bridge
          & gathered in front of the Hilton
              on Michigan Avenue at Balbo

In the lobby where the Democrats
prepared to go to the convention hall
                              four miles away
soldiers with helmets & guns
                    marched past the plush divans
                                        & the potted trees


Then, without warning, a throng of police charged the
demonstrators at 7:56
                    smashing, macing, beating
                    apparently to clear the avenue


                    Jeeps with machine guns mounted to them
                    arrived at the Hilton

"Wahoo!  Wahoo!"
        like the bomb riding cowboy
                    at the end of *Dr. Strangelove*
shouted an officer on a three-wheeled motorcycle
as he mashed into the crowd

Thus began hours of bloodshed
In the streets outside the Hilton and Convention Center
                    and it was there
                    in the surgery-room glare of the television lights--
                    that thousands took up the chant
                              "The whole world is watching
                              the whole world is watching . . ."

                McCarthy volunteers sct up
                a first aid station on the Hilton's 15th floor
                                        at his suite
                They gave up their passes
                              to get the injured up to the rooms

                Humphrey was on the 25th floor--
                    An aide opened a window and complained
                                        of tear gas

On the nominating floor four miles from the Hilton
CBS-TV's Dan Rather gave a live report,
                    "A security man just slugged me in the stomach,"

to which Walter Cronkite replied,
>               "I think
>               we've got a
>               bunch of thugs here,
>               Dan."

Inside the convention that horrible night
Senator George McGovern was a last-minute peace candidate
after McCarthy refused to lead a floor fight
>               against Humphrey

Senator Abraham Ribicoff was giving his nominating speech:
"With George McGovern," said Ribicoff, "we wouldn't have Gestapo tac-
tics on the streets of Chicago."

Mayor Richard Daley, his face reddened with malevolence,
shouted, "Fuck you, you Jew son of a bitch!
>               You lousy motherfucker, go home!"

>       Daley was seated in the front
>               Ribicoff looked down at Red Face, and said
>                       "How hard it is to hear the truth."

>               Allen Ginsberg leaped to his feet in the balcony
>               and began shouting "OMMMMM" for about five minutes
>               Meanwhile, outside
>                       in the television lights
>               the teargassed, terrified and angry crowd
>               continued its own version of ommmmm,
>               chanting, "The Whole World is Watching!
>                       The Whole World is Watching!"

(This section adapted from *1968, A History in Verse*)

## PART XVI

After the ghastly Democratic Convention
>                       in August '68
>                               in Chi
the great bard Allen Ginsberg
condensed his feelings
>               in an interview with *Playboy:*

Chicago had no government, he said,
"It's just anarchy maintained by pistol.  Inside the
convention hall it was rigged like an old Mussolini strong-arm
scene–police and party hacks everywhere illegally, delegates
        shoved around and kidnapped, telephone lines cut."

        He spent the rest of the year
        at his farm in Cherry Valley, NY
                    (not far from Cooperstown)

        They were good months.  There was
                        plenty of organic produce,
        no electricity,
                    and he built a meditation room in the attic.

        Over the years he attracted an entire generation of
                            poets and the creative
                    to the Cherry Valley area–
        so much allure there was in his soul-mind.

His book *Planet News* came out
                    from City Lights that fall

        He bought a pump organ
        & spent the Cherry Valley winter
            (& wow does it get cold up there!)
                    writing melodies to William Blake

Readers will recall Ginzap's '48 auditory "Vision" of
        Blake chanting "Ah, Sunflower, Weary of Time"
                        & "The Sick Rose"
                    in a tenement in Harlem
        spiritual experiences
                    that profoundly affected his verse.

He turned to the "prophetic simplicity"
                    of Blake's songs
after the "Police State shock despair" of Chicago.

The fine keyboard man Lee Crabtree,
                who had been in the Fugs
            visited the farm and showed Allen
                    how to transcribe his melodies.

Once that fall Ginzap drove to Woodstock
where he sang his version of Blake's "Grey Monk"
with members of the Band
                at Big Pink.

## CRACKDOWN ON UNDERGROUND PRESS

Ginsberg had begun his multi-decade investigations
                                into the secret police
There was an extensive network of what they called
                                Underground Newspapers
                all over the States—

Around October of '68
a CIA Chaos (Civilian Disruption) Agent
        (Chaos was a disruption program against the
                                anti-war movement)
whacked out a memo which noted
        "the apparent freedom and ease in which filth,
        slanderous and libelous statements
        and what appear to be almost treasonous
                anti-establishment propaganda
                        is allowed to circulate"
                                in underground papers.

The CIA smut-sleuth then suggested a strategy for silencing
the underground:

"Eight out of ten," he wrote, "would fail if a few phonograph record
companies stopped advertising in them."

The CIA of course denies it directly carried out the concept of
interdicting the record company moolah stream—

Instead the FBI did it.  In January of '69 the San Francisco
office of the Bureau
                wrote to headquarters
                        that Columbia Records
                                by advertising in the Underground
                "appears to be giving active aid and comfort to enemies
                                of the United States."

The memo suggested the FBI persuade Columbia Records
            to stop advertising in the underground press

        It worked.
        By the end of the next year
        many record company ads had been pulled
        & a number of undergrounders had folded


    Ginsberg sniffed this crackdown out
            and spent years researching it

        finally supervising a book, based on his
        research, for the PEN American Center

    called *The Campaign Against the Underground Press.*

### MARCH 12, 1969

        Ginsberg (and Kerouac too) kept everything
        doodles on napkins
            drafts of poems, bus tickets,
                            you name it

        On March 12, Allen began shipping the many
        boxes of his papers
    from his dad's attic in Paterson
            to the special collections department
            at Butler Library, Columbia U.

                    •

Allen's melodies to Blake
            revealed another of his Muse skills:
he was good at shaping melodies–

        The Fugs had done some recording
        at Apostolic Studios
                    at 39 East 10th
        with an engineer named David Baker

We liked what he did
and so when Allen Ginsberg wanted to record his
                    settings of William Blake
I recommended Apostolic

The summer of '69
  when Allen recorded there–
he had some fine musicians to help–

Julius Watkins, who had played with the Thelonius Monk Quintet,
          on French horn
Elvin Jones played drums on some of it

Charles Mingus recommended Herman Wright on bass

Don Cherry breathed some hot trumpet & percussion
      onto the oxide-dappled tape.

    All total Allen recorded 19 Blake tunes
      that June & July
   which were released, as they say,
      by M-G-M Records in 1970

     •

In October of '69
  Allen was just about to leave for a poetry tour
      beginning with Yale
    & then a teach-in about Vietnam
        at Columbia U

He was up at the farm
Gregory Corso
  had come for a visit

It was the night of October 21
  the phone rang
    Gregory answered,
      it was the writer Al Aronowitz

    He turned to Ginsberg–
"Al! Jack died."

Early the next morning
Ginsberg and Corso
    walked through the early snow
    to the woods up the hill
     & carved Jack's name
       in a tree

## PART XVII

Kerouac was watching *The Galloping Gourmet*
eating some tuna & sipping whiskey
                    in his living room
jotting in a notepad
            when the blood burbled up his throat.
            He never regained consciousness


Allen wrote a beautiful poem, "Memory Gardens"
after Jack's funeral
            with the lines
            "I threw a kissed handful of damp earth
                    down on the stone lid
                        & sighed
                    looking in Creeley's one eye,
            Peter sweet holding a flower . . ."

& ending with:

            "Well, while I'm here I'll
                    do the work–
            and what's the Work?
                    To ease the pain of living.
            Everything else, drunken
                        dumbshow."


                        •


The fall of '69 saw John and Yoko's
                Bed-In for Peace
                    in Canada

Allen was mentioned in "Give Peace a Chance"
so he called Lennon during the Bed-In
                    to give good wishes.

In early December the 'Zap testified at the ghastly
                    Chicago Conspiracy Trial

It was a rough time
Allen was subjected to what William Kunstler
depicted as "a refined form of fag baiting"
by sex-&-drug-obsessed
prosecutors

But it was probably the first & only time
mantras & the Seed Syllable Om
were ever sung in a Federal trial
plus Allen chanted from memory
much of "Howl"

•

Allen's poetry was becoming ever more imaged with
environmental issues
beginning in 1970

when he was in Philadelphia for the first Earth Day
April 22
walking with Senator Ed Muskie & thousands
on a three-mile walk
from the art museum to a park

Then 12 days later
the hideous shootings on a campus hill
at Kent State University
–the subject of Crosby, Stills, Nash & Young's
"Four Dead in Ohio."

Allen was investigating
the involvement of US agents & agencies
in the drug business
& during a meeting with former Attorney General
Ramsey Clark
A.G. learned about the FBI's sleazy campaign
against Martin Luther King

He was still fascinated by Whitman's concept
of the Fall of the nation
& was writing the verse that was to become
*The Fall of America*
*poems of these states*
*1965-1971*

Allen stayed at his Cherry Valley farm for
                much of 1970
                It was run as a commune

with a busy moil of guests & residents
                Ray & Bonnie Bremser & 3-year-old-child,
                  Peter Orlovsky & his good friend Denise Mercedes,
                Gregory Corso,
                                & oodles of visitors such as Robert Creeley
                                Ann Charters, Carl Solomon, Herbert Huncke

                a big thatch of the Best Minds crowd

## THE MARCH 1971 HELMS BET

As we have noted, Allen began researching
the drug trade
                & asking thousands of questions
                                wherever he went

Being a Jack the Clipper, Ginzap amassed
                                hundreds of clippings and articles on the subject
(a bunch of which he sent me in 1970)

It was inspired by the 1965 attempted setup of
him by Federal narcs, & by the continued troubles
                two consecutive generations were facing (Huncke,
                Corso, Burroughs
                                & then the Ken Kesey/flower child generation)
                                in their fascination with psychedelics, opiates & pot

Allen "developed information," as they say,  that the CIA
was involved in drug distribution
                                & that a CIA-operated air base at Long Cheng
                                                was being used as a dope depot
                                                                for opium running

Then, on March 4, 1971 he read with his father Louis
at the Corcoran Gallery in D.C.

At a reception beforehand Ginsberg met
the head of the Central Intelligence Agency
                                Richard Helms

Many would have fawned, bowed & quailed
   at a meeting with the great secret policeman
   who had a fascination, it later was learned,
     with CIA mind control experiments
     robowashing and programmed deeds

but Ginsberg was not afraid
and challenged Mr. Helms about CIA
     involvement in the drug trade

Helms denied it, of course,
and then they made a bet

If Allen was right about CIA/drugs
    then Helms would meditate an hour a day
    for the rest of his life

If Allen was wrong,
    he'd give Mr. Helms his bronze dorje

The liberal D.C. establishment
    was a bit miffed & horrified
      at the great bard's
        exchange with the spymaster
but it was another illuminating
     look into his soul–

Seven years later C. L. Sulzberger of *The New York Times*
wrote the 'Zap a letter:

"Dear Allen,
 I fear I owe you an apology. I have been reading a succession of
pieces about CIA involvement in the dope trade in South East Asia and
I remember when you first suggested I look into this I thought you were
full of beans. Indeed you were right and I acknowledge the fact plus
sending my best personal wishes.
       Cy Sulzberger"
       (4-11-78)

As far as I know, Allen never attempted
   to get Mr. Helms to start
      a daily meditation practice

# PART XVIII

We left the tale of the great bard Allen Ginsberg
    in March of 1971
when he made a bet with the spymaster Richard Helms
        in D.C.
  that the CIA had been involved
      in drug trafficking
        in Southeast Asia

Pshaw! Pshaw! sputtered the wry spy guy
but Ginsberg was correct
    (and out of it came his marvelous tune, later,
        the great "CIA Dope Calypso")

The seventies had begun
    & the Bard was as famous as ever
        on his 45th birthday June 3

By '71's end he'd written 575 pages of verse
      he later placed in his *Collected Poems*

The spring of 1971 he spent in California
      where, in May, he met Chögyam Trungpa

the founder of the first Tibetan Buddhist center in the USA
Tail of the Tiger, located in Vermont

(they'd met very briefly before, in India)

Trungpa urged Allen to "make up your own poems
        on the spot.
Don't you trust your own mind?"

The next night, at a benefit, the 'Zap unlocked the lid of his
little Indian harmonium
      and spontan'd forth with a 25-minute
      piece called
    "How sweet it is to be born here in America."

Thus had begun in verse
      what Kerouac had long ago urged,

bebop level spontaneity
                    grounded in Mind

(I know from firsthand experience A.G.'s genius
at spontaneous verse–in the spring of 1966
when the Fugs were recording their second album
one night we made up spontaneous verses
at a recording studio up by Lincoln Center
              I have it on tape
              –he was very very adroit
                        at the instant laying down
                                       of interesting lines)

June 30 Allen set Blake's "Tyger Tyger Burning Bright" to music
while that summer helped put together a petition
                    to the Swiss gov't to grant political asylum
                    to Timothy Leary
              on the lam after escaping from jail
              convicted for just a tiny amount of grass

The petition of 25 writers included Kenneth Rexroth,
Anaïs Nin, Ferlinghetti, Kesey, Laura Huxley, Michael
McClure, and others

## UNKNOWN BENEFACTOR

Out of the U.S. mail blue an "unknown benefactor"
sent Ginsberg a round trip ticket to India the summer o' '71

He left in September
              –he'd not been there for 9 years
and was horrified
                    at the ghastly poverty & starvation
he viewed in refugee camps
                    long lines, not enough food to be given

& huge throngs of people on Jessore Road
                              'tween Bangladesh & Calcutta
                    failing & falling & filling
                              the fire-fumed ghats
He wrote a long poem, "September on Jessore Road"
              in which he chant-sang against

> the malice-moiled powerful of the world
> > more concerned with napalm
> > > than relief of suffering

It's the final work in his book
> *The Fall of America*
> *poems of these states*
> *1965-1971*

> October 9, 1971
> was John Lennon's 31st birthday
> & he and Yoko Ono were in Syracuse, NY.

> The day before the great album
> > *Imagine*
> > > had been released

Allen visited them at their hotel room that night
> > for a party

Jonas Mekas filmed it
Allen on harmonium & finger cymbals, Lennon on guitar
Phil Spector & Klaus Voorman also on guit's
> doing the kind of thing so easily done
> > in those days
> > a jam session consisting of
> > mantras, Blake's "Nurse's Song,"
> > and then a medley of Lennon/Beatles
> > including "Yellow Submarine"
> > > & "Give Peace a Chance."

•

That fall also Ginsberg and Peter Orlovsky read at NYU's
> > Loeb Student Center
on the south side of Washington Square

Allen, still surging with Trungpa's urging
> > to go Spontaneous
created a poem on the spot
> > that lasted an hour, titled
"Why write poetry down on paper
> when you have to cut down trees to make poetry books"

Unknown to the Bard,
Bob Dylan & David Amram
                were standing in the back of the hall,
                digging the spont'-riffs

Dylan and Amram
                came over to Ginsberg's pad later that night
where they jammed
                with Amram on his famous French horn,
                Dylan on a Guild
                & the 'Zap on harmonium

(Dylan gave him some chord lessons
                so that Ginsberg discovered he
        could improvise in a 12-bar blues format
                                        –Lightbulb!)

## THE RECORD PLANT SESSIONS

This lead to some memorable recording sessions
                        beginning on November 9, 1971
at the Record Plant in NYC

Dylan brought a pal from Woodstock with him
the singer/guitarist Happy Traum.
Also on the sessions were Jon Sholle, David Amram, Ginsberg,
        and a number of poets
                including Gregory Corso, the Russian bard
                Andrei Voznesensky, and others

The filmmaker Barbara Rubin was on hand
and I was there too
                my book on the Manson group, *The Family,* had just
                                        been published

I remember that someone was playing on a milk crate with
wires stretched across it like a psychedelic psaltery.

There was a second session November 17
Allen improvised an early version of
                        "CIA Dope Calypso"
with Dylan on guitar

There were other tunes, including "Going to San Diego,"
an anthem urging
      everybody to go to San Diego
             and protest Richard Nixon
(after Kent State & the secret bombing of Cambodia)
—San Diego was at that time the site of the Republican Convention
            though later it was moved to Miami Beach

They also recorded Allen's "September on Jessore Road"
which he was just putting in final form
      in these temporary moments
          in the quick flow of the Seventies

# PART XIX

The poet, publisher & counterculture leader John Sinclair
had been set up for a minuscule pot bust by an undercover
      agent in Michigan
      and sentenced to "10 years for 2 joints"
It was a very very very unjust sentence.

By late 1971, John had been caged in maximum security
          for a couple of years
and was a burning cause in the counterculture.

After I'd finished my book on the Manson group
I wrote a long investigative poem called
      "The Entrapment of John Sinclair"
         tracing the Sinclair setup
which John Lennon read when it was published
      in the *Los Angeles Free Press*.

Lennon decided to do a concert in support of John Sinclair
They booked Crisler Arena in Ann Arbor
        and tickets sold out in a couple of hours.

It was an eery police state time in America—
The entire weight of Attorney General John Mitchell's
      apparatus was about to focus on Lennon
& sometimes our phones clicked and popped
      like a performance poet
        doing throat-boings

Miriam and I were living a couple of blocks from Lennon & Yoko Ono
in the West Village
and somehow our phone lines got crossed

I kept hearing this English chap trying to make calls
                              while I was on the phone
Finally I realized who it was,
                It was Lennon!
        so I complained to the phone company
        who said there was a shortage of lines
                        which caused the screw-up

    (which I found not quite believable)

The concert for John Sinclair occurred on a chilly December 10th
Ginzap began the night by singing mantrams
                    for about a half hour
            and performed one of his spontaneous poems.
Stevie Wonder had just come out with "Superstition" and
                overwhelmed the packed crowd with his
                                        rendition
The great Phil Ochs was there; I read a poem, Bob Seger performed
Jerry Rubin spoke, & others including Dave Dellinger & Rennie Davis

Phil told me that Lennon had called him to sing a song
                        he'd written about Sinclair,
He imitated Lennon's voice doing the opening lines
            "It ain't fair, John Sinclair
            Ten for 2 for smoking air"

The crowd was stunned to silence when John Sinclair spoke to
the 20,000 from a phone at Marquette Prison.

There was a party afterwards,
        and the last thing that happened
                was Allen– it was almost dawn–
                fingering chords on his harmonium &
                singing to a very sleepy Lennon & Yoko
                his long lament about suffering in India
                            "September on Jessore Road."

Lennon had told us that he was willing to do concerts
in city after city
      till the counterculture hero was set free.

55 hours after Lennon and Yoko's performance
          they let John Sinclair out of prison.

The Republicans had intended at that time to hold their
convention in San Diego
      to renominate the Nix man
& Lennon had agreed to participate
      in big demonstrations
          in San Diego
I think it was then
      that the INS, the FBI, the US Senate even
         took fierce action to toss Lennon out of the country.

## 1972

Early '72
saw a staged version
      in a theater in Brooklyn
         of the great poem "Kaddish"
which ran for a month

Allen then left for a tour of Australia with Lawrence Ferlinghetti
I remember he returned with tales of
      the Aborigines and their concept of
         "Universal Dream Time"

In May
    in Boulder, Colorado
        Allen took Buddhist refuge vows
He'd decided to place himself in the lineage of
Chögyam Trungpa,
the Tibetan Buddhist teacher
      whom he had met in '71

He loved Trungpa much in the
     way he'd loved Jack Kerouac
         as a friend & challenger

that is, one who called him to account
                    at just about every point
yet remained a friend

                    •

When Ginsberg was visiting Gary Snyder
            in Nevada City, California
he decided to call presidential advisor Henry Kissinger
                    at the White House

He got through!  Allen wanted the future Secretary of State
        to get together with peace movement leaders
        such as Dave Dellinger
                    to forge a dialogue.

Apparently Eugene McCarthy offered to host such a meeting
and Allen tried to set it up,
                but, you know, a bard can get through
                to someone like Kissinger once,
                                    but not twice.

            I recall how Allen told me
            he had these dreams about Kissinger
            which caused such anger
            that he was grinding
            his teeth down
                    as he slept!

                    •

In June there was a weird break-in at the Democratic offices
at the Watergate Hotel complex in D.C.
Some CIA-connected guys, plus a right-wing Cuban,
                    were arrested
and thus the Fates were about to unravel
                    what Nixon was trying to weave

Ginsberg went to Miami with Peter Orlovksy
            to commit civil disobedience
at the Republican Convention (moved there from San Diego)

He had prepared an ambitious collection of verse,
            *The Fall of America (Poems 1965-1971)*
                    one of his finest books

& it was about to be published in late '72
                    to win him the National Book Award

## 1973

Early in the year  the 'Zap
            fell on ice at his Cherry Valley farm
and broke his leg.   A few weeks later, April19-21,
Miriam, daughter Deirdre (then 8), and I
                            visited A.G. at the farm

As we wended our way o'er very rural road-ruts
in our Land Rover
I spotted A.G. sitting in a reclining aluminum chair
in bibbed overalls and leg cast
            by the driveway

He was writing some short poems he called
"Annotations to Amitendranath Tagore's Sung Poetry."

Just as we arrived he jotted:

            "Right leg broken, can't walk around
            visit the fishpond to touch the cold water,
            tramp through willows to the lonely meadow across the brook—
            here comes a metal landrover, brakes creaking hello."

He read it to us, hot from his bard-eye.
We spent a couple of days there.
Part of the fun was going with Allen to a farm auction
We went rock-hounding in nearby road cuts
                        for Devonian fossils &
Miriam & Allen cooked a groovy stir-tossed dinner
of asparagus/Chinese mushrooms/onion chunks/ ginger/oil
            in a huge iron frying pan
                a repast that A.G. had learned  from Gary Snyder

On Easter afternoon
        we drove the pain-legged bard back down to
            his apartment in the Lower East Side
            with his cast arest on a round-topped trunk
                we'd bought at the auction

# PART XX

## 1973

When Miriam, I and Deirdre
had visited the great bard Allen Ginsberg
we'd found him in an introspective mood
        after breaking his leg on the ice at his
                farm in Cherry Valley

He did seem more subdued
                & he was in pain

He had just been inducted, with Kurt Vonnegut,
into the very prestigious
            American Academy of Arts & Letters

It was the months of the Watergate mess
and it slowly was becoming apparent
            that Nixon might come to justice.

Because of John Lennon's 1971 concert for John Sinclair
& his general antiwar stance
        the forces of Attorney General John Mitchell
        tried to toss him out of the country
        though he was living here legally

They reached back to a small pot bust in England
as an excuse

Lennon brought his energy & vast international clout
(plus his big financial resources)
           to organize an impressive defense

Allen did what he could to assist Lennon
and during that year he also worked his network
        to defend Timothy Leary who had at long last
        been seized by the U.S. in Afghanistan,
            after a long flight from
            another minuscule pot bust
               that had 'shroomed
               in police state stupidity
                  into a big deal

It was also the year Abbie Hoffman was busted,
                  charged with dealing
& energy was poured forth to help him also.

Thriving in the chaos-moil, Allen went on a long tour of Europe
                still on crutches, leg in a cast

His new collection, *The Fall of America,*
        *Poems 1965-1971*
            was getting the type of attention & praise
            that bards tremble to receive

## THE CIA/KISSINGER OVERTHROW

Meanwhile, before he could be bye-byed
Nixon, plus Henry Kissinger and the military-industrial-surrealists
              in their serial aggression
organized a coup against the elected leftist gov't in Chile

On September 11, CIA-backed military men
      attacked the presidential palace and
          killed  the elected president of Chile
                Salvador Allende

It was a time of evil.
When the great Pablo Neruda died a few days later
       the new right-wing nut government of Chile
             would not allow a public funeral

Ginsberg had been a friend of Neruda's
         and mourned.
         He vowed to try to have Kissinger imprisoned
           if Nicanor Parra or any of his other
           Chilean friends
             should come to evil.

Another great poet died also around that time
     W. H. Auden on September  28
          A.G. & Auden had not long ago read together
              in England
It was adding up.
It wasn't so much Time's Wingéd Chariot
but the whack-whack-whack of the Scythe Man
            in the time-track

& the futility of it all
        that pointed the bard toward
                meditation & an actual religious practice.

He was about as famous as a bard can be
but it was a different fame than that gi'en poets
           more belovéd by the people
           such as, say, John Greenleaf Whittier
                      or Robert Frost

It was the fame of turbulence, of an acid-age Sappho,
or a Whitman without the 19th century constraints
                of jail-risk & censorship

So, the great bard turned to
        Vajrayana Buddhism
        & the teachership of Chögyam Trungpa

      Ginsberg took part in a 3-month retreat near
      Jackson Hole, Wyoming, in late 1973
      He sat many hours a day
           sorting through his rich
              mind-river

      & wrote a lot
           including "Mind Breaths"
      which would be the title verse
           for his book of 1978

## 1974

Ginzap won the well-deserved National Book Award
    for *The Fall of America,*
        *Poems 1965-1971*

    –with some fine poems,
    including "Wichita Vortex Sutra"
    & the poem about calming the Hells Angels in the fall of '65
                        at Ken Kesey's
    & the elegies to Neal Cassady
        & Che Guevara
           & Frank O'Hara

& I can't not mention the poem
    "Consulting I Ching Smoking Pot
    Listening to the Fugs Sing Blake."

It was about the only major literary
award Allen received
He always hankered for more–
        the Pulitzer and, say, the Nobel Prize
though he was just a tad too, uh, erotic
      for the long-sought phone call from Stockholm.

Once we were talking about the MacArthur Fellowships,
and the 'Zap brought forth a kind of high-pitched, anguished,
c'mon! tone to his voice:
      "I want one of those!"

•

Meanwhile Chögyam Trungpa
    wanted to open a Buddhist poetry school
    in Boulder, Colorado

    & asked Allen, Anne Waldman, & others
             to help him

It was the summer of Nixon's famous farewell
        helicopter trip
        cleansing the White House

& there was a mote of hope in the nation.

Allen & Anne Waldman
      became the cofounders of the school
but what to name it?
Anne came up with the Gertrude Stein School
   –probably in the long term
        a better name, though not
        without drawbacks
but A.G. wanted a Kerouacian symbolism
      and Anne summoned what was to be:
    The Jack Kerouac School of Disembodied Poetics
    which had its first
        summer session in '74.

This was the same summer A.G., Peter Orlovksy
& Orlovsky's friend Denise Mercedes worked on his cottage
      at Kittkidizze
            in the gold country
                  of Nevada City in northern California
   on property next to Gary Snyder

## 1975

In the spring of '75
Bob Dylan was back in New York
          with a kind of '64-'65 hard edge
             hanging out in Greenwich Village clubs

His album *Blood on the Tracks*
          had been a big success.

After the summer he decided to go on the road
    in a bus
        with friends

Bass player Rob Stoner he charged with setting up a band.
And he invited Joan Baez, his
        friend from the early '60s

The concept grew
      to include security guys, advance workers
(who go in advance to every place where a
              concert will happen
to set up hotels, meet with concert hall staff,
            work the media
      et alia multa)

D. had decided to make a movie
Sam Shepard was brought aboard
        to write spontaneous scripts

At 4 A.M. one morn Dylan called Ginsberg
      & invited him to join the
      tour

Allen got Dylan's permission

to invite William Burroughs
                but W.B. wasn't about to
                get sucked into the
                        chaos/coke/chasm
                        of a mid-'70s rock & roll flow.

# PART XXI

We left  our tale of the great bard Allen Ginsberg
in the fall of 1975

when he was invited by Bob Dylan to
                join the Rolling Thunder Review

It was ten years since Dylan had given Allen
the money to purchase a fancy Uher tape recorder
with which he wrote his brilliant
                        "Wichita Vortex Sutra"

Allen continued his awed perception of Mr. Dylan
and was flattered
                to be asked aboard the Thunder

It was organized in secrecy
Apparently not even the musicians knew
what town they would play in
                        till the day of the gig

There were many musicians
who performed in segments,
                and then all came onstage for the finale:
"This Land is Your Land"

And so it began.
On November 3, after a few concerts,
Ginsberg, Dylan, Sam Shepard, Peter Orlovsky
                        and the film crew
visited Jack Kerouac's grave in Lowell, Massachusetts
        where A.G. chanted from K.'s *Mexico City Blues*
        then he and Dylan sat cross-legged by the stone
        & composed a slow spontaneous blues
        exchanging stanzas for Kerouac
        'Zap on harmonium, Dylan on guitar.

The Rolling Thunder buses came to Madison Square Garden
December 5, 1975
for a concert
  to raise money to help free
  Rubin "Hurricane" Carter

The night before R. Thunder had performed
in the prison where Carter was being held
  for a murder he did not commit

($100,000 was raised at the Garden
and, after six more years, Carter was finally freed)

## SNOWMASS

Meanwhile, an incident occurred
at a Buddhist retreat in Snowmass, Colorado
that caused quite a stir in literary circles.

The well known American poet W. S. Merwin &
his partner, Dana Naone,
were attending what is known as a Seminary

Merwin and Naone had spent the summer at Naropa
in Boulder
  He'd given a reading with John Ashbery
  a couple of lectures, and a workshop

That fall Chögyam Trungpa invited the couple
to take part in the Seminary, which lasted three months,
from early September till around Thanksgiving 1975
at the Eldorado ski lodge, at Snowmass, about 14 miles
        northeast of Aspen.

There were from 125 to 130 in attendance.
At the Seminary about a month was spent on Hinayana,
a month on Mahayana and the final 30 days on Vajrayana

The schedule set two weeks of lectures & classes
    followed by two weeks of sitting & meditation

## A HALLOWEEN PARTY

Trungpa decided to have the group hold a party on October 31
and that everyone should wear a costume

The party was held in what Merwin described as a
"semi-dark ski-lodge dining room" of "boom-resort architecture."

The place was packed
It had a kind of Vajra-Bacchic atmosphere
There were costumes of a wide variety
including several men with
                wrathful deities painted in, on and around
                their genitals
and another, wrapped Warholishly in aluminum foil
                      as Enlightenment

Trungpa himself arrived
and not long afterwards his guards
began stripping some of the revelers.

W. S. Merwin and Dana Naone had danced for a while
                then returned to their room.

Trungpa asked for his "assistants" to go fetch them.
They didn't want to come down.
Several hours of negotiations ensued.
Finally the guru ordered his guards
                to break and enter.
They smashed into the room
Merwin defended himself with a broken beer bottle
They were dragged before Mr. Trungpa
where there were angry words 'tween the poet, his partner
and the guru.
Several others spoke up.  Trungpa punched one of them in the face
and his assistants, who had been given the
baleful name "Vajraguards"
                stripped Merwin & Naone.

It was a famous literary event, in that
the telling of it percolated though
                literature-land for a number of years.

Ginsberg was not at the Seminary
but was caught in the moil of its repercussions
because the alcoholic Trungpa was his teacher.

In the world of the Beats, however,
            it was probably to be considered a minor event
and to be ascribed to the paths of Crazy Wisdom
though to many it was an moment of semifascist infringement.

## 1976

Early in the year
Allen had to leave the Rolling Thunder Review with
the very bad news that his 80-year-old poet father,
Louis, had been diagnosed with pancreatic cancer.

Always a family man, Allen rushed to his father's aid
"Don't ever grow old," was Louis' advice. Louis required
constant care, but it appeared as if he would survive for a while.

February 3 was Ginzap's 50th birthday.
In March he taught a course at Naropa
            in the poetry of Charles Reznikoff

## RECORDING WITH JOHN HAMMOND

In June the bard began recording with producer John Hammond
who'd done primal sessions for
            Bob D. and Bruce Springsteen

The 'Zap
    unafraid and unhesitant as always
    brought Hammond the improvised blues from the '71 Dylan dates
    plus his settings of Blake
            & a copy of his book *First Blues*

Hammond produced 8 new songs in the June sessions
which, with the tunes from the Dylan sessions,
            were enough for an album.

Columbia, in its beneficence,
            coughed up an advance of $3,000

plus paid session rates for the musicians involved
(Arthur Russell, Jon Sholle, David Mansfield,
& a young man on recorder from Glassboro State College in
           NJ named
                 Steve Taylor
who was to become very important in the bard's
                       experiments in music
                            the next 21 years)

•

Allen was teaching at Naropa the next month–
                        America's Bicentennial
when July 8 a horrible call that Louis had passed away in his sleep.

On the plane to NY the bard unhooked the bellows
                    of his little rose-hued harmonium
and composed a blues in Louis' memory,
               on "Father Death, I'm flying home . . ."

(There's a beautiful version on one of Allen's CDs, with Steven
Taylor singing exquisite harmony)
His father's death, his 50th year, the
                thock! thock! thock! of the Scythe Man
         everywhere evident
Ginsberg took on the blues of his harmonium
for a few months, feeling "finished as a poet,"
              he wrote to Gregory Corso.

Feeling finished, but not finished
because he had three books in the works:
the new City Lights collection *Mind Breaths*
plus *The Collected Correspondence of Allen Ginsberg and Neal Cassady*
and the Grove Press edition of *Journals Early Fifties Early Sixties*.

A manic genius metabolism just can't
            cease however blue the
               Scythe Man sings.

# PART XXII

We noted in our previous section
how the great bard  Allen Ginsberg
            was hearing the sad thock! thock! thock!
of the Scythe Man

who had taken his father in July of '76
& left the bard
            who was always very sensitive to the
            art form known as the blues

singing the Father Death Blues

That fall Jimmy Carter was elected president &
the uptight U.S. climate relaxed
                        just a tad
with the war finally ended
& the nightmare of the hostages in Iran
                                    years ahead

Allen Ginsberg
            now in his fifties
                        kept up his complicated balance
of research, writing, actual Buddhist practice, founding a school,
coping with his eros,
            & singing now, always, the High Metabolism
                                    Gotta Roam Blues
            (a midlife variety of his "Father Death Blues")

These were the years he
was formally investigating the activities of
                        the FBI & intelligence agencies.

(The reader will recall how A.G. in the '60s
& early '70s did historic research in
            the connection between the CIA
            & drug smuggling from Southeast Asia.
            There was his famous bet with CIA
            chief Richard Helms of 1971.)

An attorney named Ira Lowe in D.C. helped Allen

and others (including myself)
>                    get some of their secret files

## F. O. I. L.

Though some complain that it's still difficult to get their files
one of the marvels of America is
>                    The Freedom of Information Act of 1966
which requires that the records of U.S. government agencies
be made available to the public.
The law states that such information must be made available
within ten working days as a rule
>                    to the person requesting it.

The law exempts nine classes of information including
some related to national security

The F.O.I.L. was amended by the Privacy Act of 1974, which requires
federal agencies to provide individuals with any information in their files
relating to them and to amend incorrect records.

>                    Wow.

It was this law that A.G. used to sail into the
>          haunts of the secret police to examine its campaign
>          in the 1960s which effectively
>                    wiped out the Underground Press movement

Allen amassed a big collection of FBI and government documents.
He worked with the writers/editors group called PEN
and its Freedom to Write Committee
>                    to present this research to the public
>                    —a project he called "Smoking Typewriters"

## READING WITH LOWELL

February 23, '77 Allen read with Robert Lowell
>          for the Poetry Project
>                    at St. Mark's Church in NYC
Since Lowell had enormous stature
>                    in the academic world
the reading gave Allen

a sense of well-tuned satisfaction,
as he said at the time:
> "What this means is that people won't be able
> to attack me so easy anymore
> because I'm, in a sense, protected by his regard.
> If he's willing to read on the same platform with me
> & say I wrote a masterpiece –*Kaddish*– it means
> I can't be considered a barbarian jerk,
> > which is what I've been having to listen to
> > > year after year."

It was a famous reading and the great Lowell,
who had once, in 1965, declined to attend
a White House arts festival because of the war,
was so soon to pass away, age 60,
> on September 12

## LUNCH WITH COUNTERINTELLIGENCE CHIEF

> I had a chat on the phone with The 'Zap
> on April 25, '77
> He said he had picked up from Ira Lowe some of my
> FBI files,
> > one of which indicated the Bureau had
> > Miriam's and my pad on Avenue A (in the '60s)
> > > under surveillance
> > since, for instance, it described how once I left the house
> > & entered an automobile.

> He and Peter Orlovsky had recently lunched
> with the legendary former CIA counterintelligence chief
> > James Angleton

Angleton, whose cover was blown as director of counterintelligence
in fine reportage by Seymour Hersh in *The New York Times* back in '74
(Angleton complained later to Hersh that his wife
> had no idea for 31 years he was the feared
> > counterchief
> and as a result had left him!)
> had been forced from his job.

Anyway, by the time Peter Orlovsky & Ginsberg had lunch with him
the superspy was working on a book, Allen told me,
& quite anecdotally fluent.

Angleton told Ginsberg he had ordered Ezra Pound into the
Pisan tiger cage in '45 to keep him from being killed
                                        by Partisans.

At the time Allen was researching the names of
those whom the FBI & CIA had sent into U.S. domestic groups
such as the Panthers
                to sow dissension
                        under Cointelpro or Chaos.

Angleton, a lifelong friend of T. S. Eliot,
gave A.G. the name of a deputy director of the FBI
who, he said, held a master list of provos & informers.

                        •

The PEN Center report was published in 1981
                        by City Lights Books
under the title *Unamerican Activities*, and included
Ginsberg's "Smoking Typewriters"
and other essays on the activities of the secret police
                        to stifle the alternate & underground press.

                        •

That summer I taught a monthlong class in
Investigative Poetry
                at the Naropa Institute in Boulder.

The class voted to work together on a single
poetic investigation
                & to my surprise
                decided to take a close look at

the incident between the poet W. S. Merwin, his
mate Dana Naone, and Chögyam Trungpa & his
vajraguards
                that had occurred at a Buddhist retreat
                in Colorado on Halloween '75.

For a month the class conducted interviews
& searched for the truth
                        by creating a composite weave
                of statements from those who
                        had observed the event & aftermath

The result was a book, fabled in its time, titled
*The Party, A Chronological Perspective on a Confrontation
at a Buddhist Seminary.*

To his credit, Allen did nothing whatsoever to
hinder the research
        though it pained his heart.

# PART XXIII

We left our history of the great bard Allen Ginsberg
      in the summer of 1977

      when he was supervising an investigation
      of the activities of the FBI and the CIA
      and other intelligence agencies

      against the antiwar and Underground Press movements

      As we have noted he secured the services of
      attorney Ira Lowe in D.C.
      to help poets get their files

      (Lowe obtained some of mine for instance)

Ginsberg was at the level of Blizzard Fame
The letters, phone messages, knocks on the doors,
manuscripts demanding book blurbs,
            blizzarded in to Box 582
            Stuyvesant Station
            NY, NY 10009

      In the late summer/fall of 1977 Ginsberg worked
      on his next book for City Lights, *Mind Breaths Poems 1972-1977*
      with some excellent poems, "Don't Grow Old,"
      (about his father)
      "Ego Confession," plus a high-energy
      poem about being mugged
      on East 10th
            in which he was probably the only
            person in the history of

Lower East Side muggery
to have chanted "Om Ah Hum"
o'er and o'er during the mugging,
and in the book another fine poem
                    "Contest of Bards"

•

There was never a bard with so many friends
& so many humans whom he animated

He had circles in France
Circles in Italy
Circles in LA
Circles in Boston
There were Circles from his visits to India
Circles in China! &

◯'s
            all through Eastern Europe!

all swirling in his retentive mind
                    like living hieroglyphs

Most of them felt DIRECTLY connected to him
and they all wanted action!

•

October of '77
he was in the air on the way
to a symposium called "LSD: A Generation Later"
        at UC Santa Cruz

and dropped a hit in the plane
            thinking about the CIA & LSD.
Later at the symposium
he told what he had done and asked
"Am I, Allen Ginsberg, the product of
one of the CIA's lamentable, ill-advised, or
triumphantly successful
            experiments in mind control?"

•

There comes a time in the
Glut of 20th-century Stuff that a bard

especially a pack rat like Allen
HAS TO ACHIEVE SOME SORT OF
                    Zenification of the data chaos!

The 'Zap kept everything
        doodles on napkins
                gigantic blizzards of incoming mail

He had moved to a building at 437 East 12th street
                            near Avenue A and Tompkins Park
where he had taken two apartments on the
        same floor and connected them

The result was a complex of small rooms
that served him well

He finally had walls for bookshelves; a room where all the
tapes of his readings were organized (he
taped EVERY single reading--there must have
                    been thousands of cassettes)

Around this time the poet Bob Rosenthal
became Allen's personal secretary
Rosenthal in the coming years
                made Allen's ever increasing bardic burdens
                possible to endure

        otherwise Ginzap could have wound up like the old
        coot I once read about whose
        cabin was entirely filled with a giant string ball
                            he had created

because for Ginsberg, even though he had stored
many boxes of archival material at the Columbia U library

the Bard Blizzard
        had become nearly overwhelming!

Students at Naropa by now were typing his notebooks
but there were those mail sacks from the Globe!

Once around this time I visited Ginsberg and
he asked me what I did with all the magazines and books and
galleys wanting book blurbs that arrived

I said I stored them chronologically.  He lowered his voice,
almost as if he were admitting a crime,
his voice just about a whisper, and said
                    "I've started throwing some things away. It's
                    just too much."

                                •

He began focusing on teaching
–transmitting his studies of William Blake for instance
He and I shared a passion for the study of metrics
            and Allen compiled a study list on the
                            complicated ancient Greek & Latin metrics
In addition he created Beat Generation reading lists
to formalize a canon
He knew how important the
                    Battle for Space in the Textbooks would become.

His Buddhist practice continued
He created a place to meditate and to
                    do prostrations
                            at his new pad on East 12th.

                                •

Ginsberg performed in Woodstock, NY  in December of '77
with Peter Orlovsky, Happy Traum & a
            young man named Steven Taylor
            whom he'd met at Taylor's New Jersey college in '76
It was amazing.  Taylor had a beautiful high tenor voice
and could follow Allen's vocal phrasing as
                        adroitly as a ventriloquist!

& those of us in the audience at the Woodstock Artists Association
were astounded
at how Taylor's harmony floated
        in a kind of mystic perfection
        above Allen's bardic bass

For the rest of Ginsberg's life Taylor worked
with him,
            touring, recording, arranging, and
            annotating his melodies.

Allen was upset with
      never-too-brave Columbia Records
for recently declining to release the bard's album
      produced by John Hammond

      Allen told me at the time that a Columbia executive
said "Ginsberg, you're shaking
      your putz out there
          in front of everybody" &

"What if William Paley heard it?"
      was another comment
(Paley was the founder of CBS)

The album had such classics as
"Everybody's Just a Little Bit Homosexual,"
      "Hard-on Blues"
        & "CIA Dope Calypso."

      John Hammond's comment on the project:
          "It's absolutely brilliant"

      •

      Allen spent the winter of '77–'78 at his Cherry Valley farm

though I note that in January o' '78
he came out on stage one night
      improvising poetry at an Iggy Pop concert.

That year
Ginzap taught a line-by-line course on William Blake's
          *The Book of Urizen*

      (after Allen passed away, I heard that
      the transcriptions of his various lectures on Blake
      at Naropa were something like 2,000 pages long)

Allen began to focus on the Rocky Flats nuclear plant near Boulder
where they built the plutonium triggers
          for the Bomb
Plutonium had leaked out into nearby ground water.

1978 was a big year for the anti-nuke movement.
It was reflected at Rocky Flats by ongoing demonstrations
particularly at the railroad tracks leading into the place

In June of '78 Allen
        wrote his antinuke/antibomb "Plutonian Ode"
& less than a day after finishing it
he was arrested for blocking the railway
               at Rocky Flats.
At the court hearing where he entered a plea
he read the poem to a crowded room
then returned to the tracks
       –a group of protesters had put up a tepee on the ties–
              & was arrested a second time.

## PART XXIV

We left our history of the great bard Allen Ginsberg
in the summer of 1978 when
he was arrested at Rocky Flats
      released
      then returned to be arrested again
      the same day

    blocking the railcars of plutonium
    coming in to build the triggers of doom.

•

November 30-December 2
saw the great Nova Convention
      in New York City
      honoring William Burroughs
There was a wide variety of performers
including John Cage, Merce Cunningham,
Brion Gysin, Laurie Anderson, myself,
Anne Waldman, Frank Zappa, Philip Glass
   & others
      including Robert Anton Wilson
      & Timothy Leary

to celebrate the shy-bold humorist
and space prophet from St. Louis.

•

Two books in '78:
  *Mind Breaths*
and a book of his correspondence
                              with Neal Cassady

•

In February 1979
the National Arts Club gave Allen its Gold Medal
for his lifetime achievement in poetry

at the club headquarters on Gramercy Park South
with the great Ted Berrigan as master of ceremonies

Luminous minds of many sorts were on hand
such as John Ashbery, who said,
        "I think he's changed the role
        of the poet in America. Now everybody
        experiences poetry. It's much closer to us now
        than it was twenty years ago.  And I think
        that is due not only to his poetry
                but to his truly exemplary way of living."

Allen toured in the spring through Europe
with Peter Orlovsky and Steven Taylor
        By now Taylor was the musical firmament
        on which the 'Zap rested

        Taylor brought Allen's songs
                        to art
        with his close-cropped harmonies
        & his skills at arranging

That summer Allen taught a course at Naropa
that went line by line
        through Wm Blake's "Vala, or the Four Zoas"

In the fall he toured Europe again for several months
in those exhilarating/exhausting
                cycles of the thrill of performance

only to return to his New York office
& Glutted Mountains of mail and duty!
in what Thomas Carlyle called the
"Dry-as-Dusts"

The politics of America of course impinged
upon its most political of bards

Back in July of '79
The Sandinista National Liberation Front
had tossed out the creepy Somoza family dictatorship
(in place since 1934)

The Sandinistas nationalized some industries
& right-wingers around the world rolled their eyes
in Domino-Theory dread.

During those months the slow-building stage was hauled into place
that led to the Contras
Irangate
& the continuing involvement of
CIA clients with big-time drug trafficking

Another big crisis was the November 4 seizure of 66 U.S. embassy
employees
in Tehran by students

who demanded the return of the Shah of Iran for trial.
(The Shah was in the United States for cancer treatment)

President Carter was perceived as "weak" for his handling,
especially when the attempt on April 24, '81,
to rescue the hostages failed.

Ginsberg's bardic sniffing skills
were sniffing
a right wing drift
& he didn't dig it

•

Meanwhile his guru, Chögyam Trungpa,
had encouraged the bard to consider
wearing a suit and tie
so as to get a more serious
hearing from his audiences.

Allen's haberdasheries were the various Goodwills
                          in the cities he visited
and soon he began to sport
                    white shirts, ties and suit coats.

I chuckled at the emphasis on suits and ties
recalling how I'd seen the great 'Zap
back in 1959, and then in '60
          at poetry readings
                    wearing the same shirt
          & it wasn't clear if it had been
                          given a intervening wash

                    •

Added to the moil in Nicaragua & Iran
was the Soviet invasion of Afghanistan

where there had been a Marxist coup in 1978
          followed by the kind of shooting &
          clique-kill confusion
that led to a Soviet invasion
          in December of '79.

This gave the CIA and other clandestine services
the chance
          to intervene secretly against the Russians
                    in a long & hounding war

a legacy that's still not very well understood
(& will not be till
          the activities of the CIA & Reagan's CIA director Wm. Casey
          are fully explicated.)

Carter was battered by it
          especially when he stupidly refused
          to allow American athletes to compete
                    after training all their lives
                    in the 1980 Moscow Olympics

## 1980

And so, when 1980 blossomed in the Time Garden
Allen Ginsberg faced
        an uncertain American future–

After all, had he not won the National Book Award
      for a tome titled *The Fall of America?*

Thanks to Steven Taylor in the main
Allen began to write Public Poems
        with Music
            on political themes

a pattern he continued all the way to his passing in 1997

Political Poems with Music for 1980 include
    "Birdbrain" and
        "Capitol Air"

1980 saw Allen compose one of the century's finest
             environmental poems:
his "Homework
    –Homage Kenneth Koch"

with its startling series of lines
        on what it would be like to clean up
        the earth's polluted air & waters,
              beginning

"If I were doing my Laundry I'd wash my dirty Iran
I'd throw in my United States, and pour on the Ivory Soap,
    scrub up Africa, put all the birds and elephants back in
    the jungle,
I'd wash the Amazon river and clean the oily Carib & Gulf of
    Mexico,
Rub that smog off the North Pole, wipe up all the pipelines
    in Alaska,
Rub a dub dub for Rocky Flats and Los Alamos, Flush that
    sparkly Cesium out of Love Canal
Rinse down the Acid Rain over the Parthenon & Sphinx....."

& flowing onward with startling images
   –It's worth finding and memorizing
      & then to take action!
    Allen would have wanted your
              action.

## MARCH 1980

*The Party* was published
   –the poetry group I'd taught at Naropa had voted
          to set it loose to the public
& it was nicely produced by Susan Quasha at
    Station Hill Press in Barrytown near Bard College.

Tom Clark also published a book on the Trungpa/Merwin/Naone
incident,
   *The Great Naropa Poetry Wars*

and so Allen was upsettedly swept up again in the moil & boil
of this matter
    for about another year
       till the literary kettle ceased to spew.

Over his shoulder the bard heard the iron clacks
       of Reagan's stern-wheel'd chariot.

Reagan showed the kind of robotic persistence
      that Democrats often lack:

He tried in '68, ping!
He tried in '72, ping!
He tried in '76, ping!
    and then in 1980, he won the nomination!

    Carter swung to the right on domestic issues
    He refused to support Senator Edward Kennedy's
    historic
      Health Care for All Americans Act

    and the first real chance for a National Health Care System
    since Truman's 1948 proposal
      was shot down in
      grimy conservative-Democratic
        lack of vision

•

That year the bard received a $10,000
                    NEA Creative Writing fellowship

He'd become friends with financier George Soros
For years the bard went to the New Year's parties
                    thrown by Soros and his wife, Susan
Back in the late '70s he was worth a mere $600 million
and when Allen won the NEA
                    he called him and asked what he
                    could do with the money

Soros laughed & suggested he put it in the bank.

•

In October, the filmmaker Barbara Rubin died
of postnatal infection
            in France
                    after giving birth to her fifth child

She was a ceaseless advocate for interesting art & music
during the '60s
(She was the first one to point out to me the presence
                        of the Velvet Underground)
Barbara had located the Cherry Valley farm Allen bought
                    & can be seen rubbing Dylan's aching head
                        on the *Bringing It All Back Home* album jacket

Rubin, whose films include *Christmas on Earth,*
once hoped to settle down with Allen in Cherry Valley
later married and lived as a devout chasid
                    till the Scythe Man seized her early too early too early

•

Allen was on tour in Europe
            when someone told him the ghastly news
December 10 of John Lennon's shooting,
an event that tore out the soul
of a decade much
            as Kent State had done
                    in 1970

To Allen it was as if someone had stolen the
                    Mona Lisa's smile
            from the time-track.

# **PART XXV**

In 1981
on rising
    · he'd record his dream thoughts
      in the long gift of Jung & Freud

do prostrations
        (as part of his Buddhist practice)
then discuss his daily schedule
            with Bob Rosenthal
            the General Manager of his
            interface with the
                    gnawing public

It was a year when Ronald Reagan & th'
                        neo-cons
began the attack on the Nicaraguan Revolution

                    •

He'd returned to his two-apartment complex
on East 12 in NYC in early 1981
after a long five-country tour of Europe
            with Peter Orlovksy & Steve Taylor

He was at the age where a big one-nighter tour
                started to take what they always
                call a "toll"

–a sort of Scorch Tax
                on his physicality and his continuing
ability, to use the words of Tuli Kupferberg,
to "stay above room temperature."

                    •

He always carefully arranged the things
of his pad
        artworks, books, meditation zones
                his writing supplies

almost as minutely precisioned as, say,
Robert Creeley

●

Early in March
novelist Bill Burroughs, Jr., son of William
died in Florida
of cirrhosis of the liver
He'd had a transplant in '76
I remember him throwing up blood
in our apartment at Naropa one summer

Later, hopelessly craving alcohol,
he would sit on the floor of  the Liquor Mart
in Boulder
chugging vodka

to join the flow
of the solar system's
second generation stardust
as quickly as he could.

Allen returned to Naropa in the spring
where he taught a minutely detailed
"Literary History of the Beat Generation"

& organized Bill Burroughs, Jr.'s papers
made sure that Billy's journals were
typed into manuscript form.

As for the "Literary History of the Beat Generation"
it was duly taped
& no doubt transcripts are held in the
Allen Ginsberg Library at Naropa

Conservatives & Literary Opponents
sneered at Ginsberg often
as some sort of
barbarian invader

but in truth he was a better scholar than
just about all of them.

Time will drum this truth.
In fact, he was a great scholar
The same ferocity for accurate detail
            he brought to, say, the history
              of the CIA & heroin smuggling
                    in SE Asia

he brought to the details of
Poesie's History.

He could recite by mind
thousands of lines of verse

& knew the history of poetic things
as much as any staid professor
              in bentwood walls

How do I know this?
Read the transcripts of his essays,
              interviews & lectures
(or his 2000 collection, *Deliberate Prose*)

## JUNE 1981

The 'Zap had gone back to NYC and
            was getting ready for a long tour
when he went to a club called Bonds to
meet a group called the Clash

and went backstage to hang out

The lead singer, Joe Strummer, asked the bard
to read some poetry

Instead he proposed his po-tune "Capitol Air"
They rehearsed it
        a few minutes
             & A.G. sang it for  the 3,000 awaiting

thus adding a new-wave hero band to those with whom
he had performed (the Fugs, Phil Ochs, John Lennon,
Dylan, et alia multa)

**SUMMER 1981**

Ginsberg worked on the proofs of
*Plutonian Ode and Other Poems,*
         *1977-1980*  for City Lights

his 8th for Ferlinghetti's great House
         (if you count *Iron Horse,* published
            in tandem with Toronto's Coach House Press)

•

All these tastes of the mega-stage
           with rockers
helped him hunger to form a band.
In August, I heard from a staff member
that Ginsberg was going to call his band
           Glass of Chicken

Glass of C. apparently
was Corso's term for Shambhala

**A RETURN IN TRIUMPH**

The bard loved to return to Columbia
for triumphal readings

as if he had some sort of spot on the palm
         from his university days of the '40s

November 14, 1981
marked his third historic reading
         at McMillin Theater

for a 25th anniversary recitation of "Howl"
Was it **really** twenty five years
        since the great threnody/joy psalm
           had been published!?

Jack Kerouac who had beaten time
        on a jug of Burgundy
           and shouted "Go! Go!"
during the first performance

at the Six Gallery back in th' fall o' '55
was gone
        Neal gone
            the surge of the late '50s & '60s gone
& the nation was oozing & spewing to the right

yet the theater was packed
His family far and near had gathered
and as one person who was there has described it:
"Many luminaries, including Carl Solomon were present.
Steve Taylor accompanied Allen. . . . The audience
was literally awestruck, one of the only times
I've experienced that.  Allen made many funny asides
annotating his works
        as he read."

Thunder always thunders.

                        •

In late '81 he moved to a house in Boulder
where he was to headquarter for the next five years
            devoting himself more to the
                growth of the Jack Kerouac School
            of Disembodied Poetics
                at the Naropa Institute

& left his New York office
        under the stewardship of Bob Rosenthal

    worked on the manuscript for
        *Plutonian Ode, Poems 1977-1980*
            for City Lights

### EARLY 1982

At Jimi Hendrix' Electric Ladyland studio
                on 8th St. in the Village
the Clash were recording

Ginsberg spent a few days with them
helped write three or four tunes
        His suggestions they tested
            on empty tracks
                to gauge their flow

The bard  loved the ambience of
                successful rockers
and couldn't resist the urge to teach
bringing them Gregory Corso's newest book for instance,
and the City Lights classic *Clean Asshole Poems* by Peter Orlovsky.

The album was called *Combat Rock*
                and the bard, not always so modest
                did not ask for
                publishing royalties on the
                                tunes he helped doctor.

## JANUARY 16, 1982

Tuli Kupferberg & I got together
                with some hot musicians, including Coby Batty,
                John Zorn, Marc Kramer, Randy Hudson &
                                                Steve Taylor
to play the Mudd Club in New York City

It was not quite a reunion of the Fugs
(who had not performed since 1969)
but close enough
                & the place was utterly packed

I invited Allen to sing along with us when
we performed Tuli's great tune "Nothing"
                                from the first album of '65

Tuli basso'd forth with his traditional verses
"Monday nothing Tuesday nothing
                Wednesday and Thursday nothing. . . ."

The music was slow and properly eery
John Zorn on saxophone
                Kramer on scary organ
                                Coby Batty on hand held drum

Then Allen sang a verse
in a slow Ancient Bard voice of declination:
                "New York Nothing
                Moscow Nothing Washington D. C. Nothing
                Salvador War fooooor Nothing
                Chögyam Trungpa (pause) Buddha (pause)  Nothing"

•

Allen & Peter O flew to Nicaragua on January 21
at the invitation of the poet Ernesto Cardenal
                    (the minister of culture
                        after the Sandinista Revolution of '79)

for an international literary festival
in honor of the national poet of Nicaragua, Rubén Darío

The bard did not want to incite the kind of trouble
he had
        back in 1965
                when he had been tossed, first from Cuba
                            & then from Czechoslovakia

for this time the circumstances were very different.

Much had been learned by 1983
of what the CIA and military intelligence
                had done in Chile in the early '70s
                to destabilize & overwhelm the
                freely elected left-edged government
                            of Salvador Allende

Allen knew those intricacies, knew them well
& wanted to see for himself
                    what was going on in Nicaragua
without helping
        the harbor-miners & Contra-feeding maw
                            of the Reagan era.

It was an era of the Lie
(For instance, New York's own Senator Patrick Moynihan
resigned from the Senate Intelligence Committee
in 1985 when CIA director Wm Casey flat out lied
        under oath about the CIA mining of
                            Managua's harbor)

The Sandinista National Liberation Front that
finally overthrew the ghastly Somoza family dictatorship
was named for Augusto Cesar Sandino

<blockquote>
a great Nicaraguan patriot<br>
who was killed by Anastasio  Somoza<br>
on whose orders he was lured to an airport<br>
in Managua and offed in '34.
</blockquote>

The FSLN, as it was known, put together a broad coalition,
including business interests, to get rid of the dictatorship,

but Daniel Ortega's Sandinistas felt the opposition of the USA
from the very beginning

<blockquote>
During the festival<br>
Allen, Ernesto Cardenal<br>
    & Yevgeny Yevtushenko<br>
wrote a "Declaration of Three"<br>
which called on the "world's writers to come<br>
to Nicaragua to see with their own eyes<br>
the reality of Nicaragua, and lift their voices<br>
in defense of this country,<br>
        small but inspired."
</blockquote>

Not long after Allen and Peter returned from Managua
a CIA destabilization plan, worth $17 million in '82 dollars
oozed into the media.

•

Out in California
    where he played the legendary McCabe's
        Guitar Shop
he recorded two tunes with Bob Dylan in
        Santa Monica
as a kind of demo tape
—one tune was "Do the Meditation Rock"
    a kind of an interesting metered shuffle
    with a rushing chorus of
    *Do the meditation     Do the meditation*
    *Learn a little Patience and Generosity*

& the other was "Airplane Blues"

<blockquote>
It was always a pleasure to hear him sing "Airplane Blues"<br>
with its sum-up hook line of
</blockquote>

"Hearts full of hatred
will outlast my old age"

(Both po-tunes are in
the 'Zap's '86 book *White Shroud*)

## A TRIBUTE TO JACK

In late July/early August of '82
there was a big celebration at Naropa
to mark the 25th anniversary
of *On the Road*

So many were on hand that space had to be rented at
the University of Colorado
and at the Chatauqua complex
out by those graceful red faces
known as the Flatirons
All the complexities of the Beat/Flower Power/Rock & Roll/
Art/Movie/New Literature conspiracy were on parade

as Allen, with the same intricate high metabolism he'd
used to find publishers for his entire generation
or had organized the reading at the Six Gallery in '55

now brought to Boulder a list of humans that included
Wm Burroughs, Gregory Corso, Diane di Prima, Carolyn Cassady,
Herbert Huncke, John Clellon Holmes, Lawrence Ferlinghetti,
Carl Solomon, Robert Frank, Joyce Johnson, Ken Kesey,
Ted Berrigan just months to live, Ray Bremser, Anne Waldman,
Michael & Joanna McClure, Timothy Leary, Paul Krassner &
        Kerouac biographers
        Ann Charters, Dennis McNally, Gerald Nicosia
                                        plus Abbie Hoffman
                        & father-thirsty Jan Kerouac
                        now almost 30

        There were over 130 "accredited" as they say
        reporters on hand

        Robert Frank  filmed conversations
                                on the Chatauqua porch

where those of the Beats or Beat-touched
bumped & interacted
were introduced, or renewed antique friendships

A.G. was everywhere
  urging and coordinating
    sleeping just five a night

till it was over
  & he took to bed for three days

It made Naropa good bread
but it had cost the Bard a few thousand of his own money
but money never measures the love of a soul

It was another payout for Jack
in the lineage of
Ginzap pressuring Mark Van Doren
  on *The Town and the City*
  so that Robert Giroux
  accepted it unread from Van Doren
    & a $1,000 advance

& Ginzap coming up with the ending of *Doctor Sax*
& hundreds of other benevolences
    toward his thankless pal

## PART XXVI

### FALL 1982

That fall he attended a conference at UCLA
organized by Norman Cousins & Robert Rees
    both on the faculty

between writers from the Peking Writers Union
    and inkers from the USA
among them Arthur Miller, Gary Snyder & Kurt Vonnegut

It was the first opening of the Door
and presaged
  a visit to China, A.G. included,
    two years in the future.

## BARDING FORTH

The great Bard sailed forth for another tour of Northern Europe
    and Scandinavia
                into '83

With him was his young strong-voiced musician/singer
Steven Taylor.

It's not that easy
        to track Allen's travels
                during his final decade & a half

They say that
        cosmic rays
            are more plentiful
                up in the air

and Ginzap probably had more such rays
        bonking his noggin
            than any other bard in history

While he was barding through Europe
John Hammond let forth the double album *First Blues*
                    *1971-1981*
            on his own John Hammond Records

The reader will recall how back in 1978
the feeble-thinking & cowardly Columbia Records
        had refused to put it out
        so Hammond, the discoverer of Dylan,
                formed his own label.

There had been additional sessions in '81
and now here it was,
        24 tunes

## TO SING OR NOT TO SING

"... I know Allen will follow me around the world
        with his terrible singing voice ..."
           –Ted Berrigan
           *Ann Arbor Song*

In the matter of his music and singing
  some liked, some disliked

Some felt it detracted from his writing
   but it came from a long tradition
   going back to Archilochus
     & the choice of a bard
     to sing, to chant, to recite
     & to do all three
        in freely chosen combinations

Allen loved his voice
His phrasing was very good
     Check out "Ballad of the Skeletons"
     or the fast-metered
       "CIA Dope Calypso"

&, with Steve Taylor singing harmony
   say, on "Father Death Blues"
   or "Do the Meditation"
     it was very pleasing to see & to hear

but the 'Zap used as few chords as John Lennon
or the early Dylan
   and, as art songs,
     wend weakened in the Time Track

however brilliant the Mind & Voice
         infiring them.

## A SCHOLAR AT SONG

Steve Taylor told me how once
during the '80s
he went to the Metropolitan Opera with Allen
& the bard knew all the melodies & words
   of *La Traviata* by heart!

## PETER IN TROUBLE

As Allen and Steven Taylor toured Europe
Peter Orlovsky was set to join them
bringing his banjo & his fine skill at yodeling

yet Peter was again in sore trouble.

Always a caregiver
& attentive to the super-minutiae of healing
he'd nursed his father Oleg dying of cancer
that fall
trying to "ease the pain of living"
till November 12 he'd passed away in NYC

He arrived in Europe
      moily & erratic
           & needing care himself

& strayed beyond Beat Generation standards
for deportment on the road
      which were among the most relaxed standards
      in the history of Western culture.

## 1983

John Lennon had suggested that A.G. do "Jessore Road"
(from his 1971 tour of India
      the refugee horror on the road from
           Calcutta to East Pakistan)
with a string quartet

Steven Taylor composed it & it was recorded in Amsterdam
with the Mondrian String Quartet.

    Allen was in an interesting film called
    *Poetry in Motion*
        much of it shot in Toronto early in the year

    then he went out on a big
    tour to "support"
        the double *First Blues*

        returning to

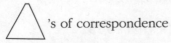 's of correspondence

•

June 3, his 57th birthday
    celebrated with his brother Eugene
        who had just turned 62

•

Burned out from Naropa he
    became codirector emeritus
    after ten years with Anne Waldman
    (and year 'pon year of flaming youth eagerness staff)
        creating probably the finest academy of its time

### AUGUST 1983

The poet of beautiful vowels
Lawrence Ferlinghetti
        & his City Lights Books
had published all of Allen's great collections

and what a March of Ink they were!!

*Howl and Other Poems*
    *Kaddish and Other Poems*
        *Reality Sandwiches*
*Planet News*
    *The Fall of America*
        *Mind Breaths*
            *Plutonian Ode*

    –25 years of
        Bardic sizzle cymbal
    in the Final Ensemble

•

This was the year he secured the services
of a young book agent
    famed for his brashness & boldness
named Andrew Wylie
who had begun his agenting in 1980
by representing the great I. F. Stone
in his book *The Trial of Socrates.*

Wylie urged the bard to publish a *Collected Poems*
with a major publisher
Allen was hesitant at first
not wanting to break his
longtime flow with Lawrence Ferlinghetti

They telephoned the author of *A Coney Island of the Mind*
and he was less than happy
so AG was ambivalent about proceeding

Then there was a breakthrough
Wylie negotiated a six-figure contract
with Harper & Row (later HarperCollins)
which allowed Ferlinghetti
to keep all of A.G.'s City Lights books in print

Harper & Row would publish a *Collected Poems*,
an annotated edition of "Howl,"
(in the way that such a book had been done
for Eliot's "Waste Land"),
a book of new poems (which was to
contain the exquisite poem "White Shroud"),
a volume of Letters,
one of Essays, and one of Journals

(Wylie, who had studied ancient Greek at Harvard,
then written for the underground papers and owned
a bookstore on Jones Street in the West Village,
w/ stints at cab driving and showing up at Max's Kansas City
in the afternoons for free fried chicken,
surged forth to become one of the most successful
of American literary agents
with around 300 clients at the
time of this writing
& offices in NY, London, Madrid, Tokyo
and perhaps other places too)

## MIRACLE DREAM

He was always a Dream Man
and so
he awakened before full light on October 5
in his apartment in Boulder

from a dream
    no Gentleman from Porlock
        would interrupt

to write one of his finest poems.
He called it "White Shroud"

It began with 10 rhymed & semirhymed couplets
the first one:
    "I am summoned from my bed
    to the Great City of the Dead"

He was walking with the great pacifist writer
        David Dellinger
It was a kind of Sheol, or Bronx Elysium

He comes across
a cranky-haired shopping bag lady sleeping on a wooden platform
        in an alley
whom he startlingly recognizes as Naomi!

    He spots
    a nearby basement store
    room where he could
  live
    & take care of her

"she needed my middle aged strength and worldly money knowledge,
housekeeping art. I can cook and write books for a living,
she'll not have to beg her medicine food, a new set of teeth
for company, won't yell at the world, I can afford a telephone . . ."

Then he awakened
in a "glow of life"

before dawn
wrote down his poem, ran out of ink
went downstairs
where Peter Orlovksy was already up

"I kissed him & filled my pen and wept."

•

I remember how A.G. had wept
reading the Crazy Jane poems of Yeats.

'56
'83

a 27 year
        flow of guilt
        for Naomi

still minyan-less
still with wires in her body
still singing the Internationale
                        from the Beyond

for a mother
        dying weirdly
                never dies.

## PART XXVII

### FALL 1983

I spoke with Allen on October 25
We chatted about many things
how to improve relations with Russia
                        for instance
& techniques he'd learned from Trungpa
                on the struggle against nukes
He mentioned he was leaving Boulder

"I'm retiring here
I'm about $10,000 in debt
because I've been sort of inert
I've got about $10,000
            in secretarial fees. . . .

[he'd not been touring since the spring]

I'm coming back to NY
       [after a few years in Boulder]
I've hired an agent, Andrew Wylie,
to peddle my books to Madison Avenue
for a standard edition of poetry & prose
about 4 volumes–collected poetry & everything.

I'm coming back to NY in December
& I'm going to try to restructure my
          whole finances."

I broke in, "I thought you did some investing with your brother—
I thought you were set up for life!"

He protested, "Oh No! NO
       I'm just living on what I make from readings
       and what I get from City Lights
           (reportedly about $7k a year)."

E.S.: "I thought you had salted away
         a lot over the years."

A.G.: "No, I've got to do it now [laughs]
       I'm going to see if I can do something
         w/ my papers at Columbia
           to get an annuity out of them
        as Robert Bertholf suggested

I have all of my stuff
        more or less intact

I sold some stuff to Columbia
Literary letters from Burroughs, Kerouac & Corso
That's the only thing missing
The *Kaddish* I gave away
        to the Living Theater
    [for a benefit auction]

They say it's worth anywhere from
200,000    500,000   a million
           nobody knows
I'm getting too old to run around now.

I'm getting more and more interested in
                                technical stuff
writing glyconics
            & things like that

[glyconics, an ancient meter as follows  ⌐υ⌐υυ⌐υ⌐ ]

Want to hear some?"

"Sure," I replied.

Then he chanted a complicated pattern of verse he'd written
in metrical couplets: the first line a glyconic
& the second in what's known as 2nd Aesclepiadean:

            ( ⌐υ⌐υυ — || ⌐υυ— υ⌐ )

        — υ — υ υ — υ —
"One deep time I could write of death
        — υ — υ υ — || — υ υ — υ — υ
Love joy God in my youth Loves in my heart I carry
        — υ — υ υ — υ—
Now new love in my age I feel
        —  υ  — υ υ — || — υ υ — υ —
Right speech come to my heart  Time for the Muse to Weep. . . ."

& other glyconic/Asclepiadean couplets
                        chanted he
                        in his thrilled-with-verse
                                voice of the Bard

    "I find it easy to do those,"
                    he said

                        •

Through Henry Geldzahler, then the NYC commissioner of culture,
and Raymond Foye, Allen met a famous young artist
named Francesco Clemente
                and his wife Alba
and began a friendship that lasted to the end.

A.G. always had a flair for design and drawing
and festooned his books at signings
            with ornate ouroboroi, skulls with flowers in the teeth,
            and many kinds of intricate inkery

The bard worked with Clemente on a remarkable & beautiful edition
of "White Shroud"

A.G. hand-inked the poem into a folio at Francesco's studio
on December 20
       and then the artist illustrated the brilliant verse
       with some thrilling watercolor figures
       including a stunning green ouroboros at the close
       where, instead of the snake holding its tail in its mouth
       a human head mouths a breast

The folio was published as a book
       for a Clemente exhibition in Basel in '94

### 1984

*The New York Times Sunday Magazine* ran "White Shroud"
       early in the year

and then on March 15 *The New York Times*
published a blacklist created by the Reagan-era
       United States Information Agency
of prominent Americans **not** to be
invited for government-funded overseas appearances—
there on the blacklist along with Ralph Nader,
Walter Cronkite, Betty Friedan and Coretta Scott King
was the great bard Allen Ginsberg!

          •

Meanwhile, the 'Zap set about creating
       a little better sense of order
          in his part of the universe

    All his life
       all the way back to the Spanish civil war
          he'd been a compulsive news clipper
    and he was also the Kodak Man!

Ann Charters had gathered some of his photos
back in 1970
    for a small collection called  *Scenes Along the Road*

but few sensed what photographic hugeness
                    lurked in the Forest Ginsberg!

    Ginsberg's photos were "on deposit" along with his gigantic archives
    at Butler Library at Columbia

    On deposit meant that they were open to scholars
                             with the bard's permission

    Over the years he'd sent people to the photos in the archives
    and sometimes the prints & negatives both wd disappear

    A.G. asked a young writer & publisher named Raymond Foye
                             to work on the photos

    Foye went to Butler Library
    & was rather horrified to see the negatives out of their sleeves
                    & scattered here and there in the boxes
    There were thousands upon thousands of
            his photographs
                    many of them still in their '40s/'50s packets
                    from the Tompkins Square Park pharmacy
                             where he'd had them developed

    Many were the large old-style negatives, 2 1/4-inch square,
    which stood the test of blow-up well

    that is, would a scrubbly-chinned, defiant Jack Kerouac
    leaning up against a Lower East Side roof-wall in 1953
                    stand the test of becoming a 11 x 14 art print?

    Foye tried to keep a chronological sense of the rolls
    putting the negatives into archival sleeves
                    creating a numbering system in 3-ring notebooks

    He ordered contact sheets from the negs

            A.G. studied the prints and contact sheets
            selecting what he liked

            He tried blowing up a few of the negs
                    onto top quality 11 x 14 paper

Brian Graham made prints of those choices
(Graham is Robert Frank's printer)

Borrowing an idea from his friend the photographer Elsa Dorfman
Allen wrote detailed histories
which he inscribed on blank space at the bottom fronts of the photos.

Foye and Allen put together a portfolio of signed prints
and Foye began to show them to galleries and dealers
The Spencer Collection at the NY Public Library
          was among those who purchased a set at $5,000

The Holly Solomon Gallery on 57th Street
          agreed to do the bard's virgin show
                    which Foye curated
                              (with an opening in early '85)

Thus was born another industry in the Forest Ginsberg:
*A.G.–Chronicler of the American Beat Generation Experience*

Up to then his cameras had been
                    not that carefully chosen & his techniques
dancing somewhere 'tween luck, Cage, & excess energy.

He pestered his pal Robert Frank
one of America's finest photographers for advice.

And met the great Berenice Abbot
who once had worked with Man Ray
A.G. dug immensely her NYC photos from the 1930s

"It was like going back in a time machine . . ."
                    he later wrote.

She urged him to get a camera with large negatives
He got Abbot to accompany him to Olden's camera store in NYC
to check out the action on a Rolleiflex
                    he was about to purchase

Another example of the bard
                    throughout his career
                              reaching out to the best minds
                                        for the best advice.

After his early negatives were blown up
                    and it was seen they were art

        the same bard who
        made his own
                big set of drums
        in the jungles of Chiapas
                        in '54
        was utterly unafraid
        31 years later
                to leap into the art of
                        the Visual Muse.


In fact, he went click-batty for a while
He shot thousands upon thousands of pictures
                        during his roamings
One person on his staff spent all her time
                keeping track of the prints


It was a visual diary:  "It's beginning to replace writing a lot,"
he wrote, "not the poetry, though, but the peripatetic notes
                                    I used to take."


At first, before the explosion of photo shows,
it was a financial drain,
        as he blew up hundreds of shots, and alternate shots
        of the same view
                to large-size prints


## HAWKING CHUCKLING AT THE EDGE

One of Allen's key assistants
during those years
was his bibliographer, Bill Morgan
        who'd worked since 1980 on a very detailed
        bibliography–it included even rounding up
                the multitude of book blurbs
                        the bard had dashed off


He started cataloging all the books in Ginsberg's apartment
Then around 1984
began work at Columbia
        "to organize those hundreds of boxes"
                        as he later described it

Around that time Barry Miles had gotten a contract
from Simon and Schuster
            to write a bio of Allen

The 'Zap worked out a deal
for Morgan to get a percentage of Barry Miles' S&S advance

so that Morgan could work full time
                        bringing order  –heh heh–
            to the "word horde"

Allen loved to feel
            as if his work were organized
                        in a retrievable, graceful
                                    raked-sand Zen Zone

(you can see it in the order he made
            in the room, say,
                        where he began "Howl"

except that apparently,
in the Universe
            you create more disorder
                        when making order of your things
according to Hawking's *A Brief History of Time*

so that if you memorized all of Bill Morgan's two-volume
bibliography of the great poet's writings
                                    for instance

you would create disordered energy in the form of heat
            from the ordered energy of food
                        lost in the air around you
                        in convection and heat

such as to increase the disorder of the Universe).

·

That year, 1984 he jumped out on
                        two little tours of Europe

and on June 4 took time to
            come to a reunion of the Fugs
                        at the Bottom Line

–you can hear his voice shout-crooning along
        on the live CD that we have left behind in the time-track.

•

    Meanwhile the commissions & contracts for this & that piled up
    Raymond Foye was smiling when he told me that
    it would take Allen fifteen minutes just
        to describe the basic array of projects
            he had to complete

Guilt was never far away from the dark-diaried bard
who seemed to savor having something lurking
        & guilt-demanding
such as sitting in a well-appointed cabin that spring of '84
at the Atlantic Center for the Arts in Florida
an easy gig as a Master Teacher yet
worrying about the introduction to his
    *Collected Poems*
        which he'd not yet finished

•

He spent the '84 summer in a Boulder town house complex
    which Naropa rented in those years for its summer faculty

and finally completed *Collected Poems 1947-1980* on July 18
837 pages of flow
    with 88 pages of notes

He quit smoking
& was swimming regularly in Boulder Creek
    which flows down from the mountains
        & across the city

At summer's end
as he prepared to face the
    impending publication of his heart's work
he wrote a fine little
    addendum to Christopher Marlowe:

"It's All So Brief"

I've got to give up
Books, checks, letters
File cabinets, apartment

pillows, bodies and skin
even the ache in my teeth.
*September 14, 1984*
(p. 57, *White Shroud*)

echoing, say,
that searing final line of loss
in Olson's *Maximus Poems:*

*My wife   my car   my color   and   myself*

# PART XXVIII

## A TRIP TO CHINA

We left our tracing of the great bard's life
with the completion of 88 pages of notes
for his *Collected Poems*

which now Harper & Row
was taking to galleys
corrections, design
& ink
& the great bard was not the sort
to wait around
eating his nails.

In October he traveled to China
with a delegation that included
Gary & Masa Snyder, Francine du Plessix Grey,
Harrison Salisbury, William Least Heat-Moon, Toni Morrison,
Maxine Hong Kingston, William Gass
for the American Academy of Arts & Letters

A.G. prepared himself by studying
the '66-'76 Cultural Revolution in China

& learned that
"I saw the best minds of my generation destroyed by madness"
meant to the Chinese those wrecked
by the Cultural Revolution

Gary Snyder
moved by the visit to Cold Mountain temple
where Han Shan had lived
Gave the monk there his '58 translations
of the Cold Mountain Poems
          and wrote some verse on the spot
          "At Maple Bridge"

As for Allen, he was shock-miffed
at the rather puritanical Chinese culture
& made sure he talked aplenty
          on sex & politics & personal freedom
He had a gig to file reports on China
          to UPI

          From Shanghai on Dec. 14
          he sent me a packed postcard:
"The Cultural Revolution here 1966-74 was like worst
elements of U.S. right _and_ 'left' takeover, bookburning,
gangs of street kids with spears going downtown to torment
old bearded scholars, etc. New Economics '4 Modernizations'
now really interesting 'open door' of Mind too. Students shy,
eager, virginal, good English, a few able to talk frankly private
thoughts.

          "Been down Yangtze Gorges on 3 day boat–& various cities,
teaching. Now on weekend vacation rainy train Shanghai to
Nanching, travel with postgraduate English student translator
interpreter whose wife had baby last week–mist & smog,
marvellous small scale farming fields along the R.R. line, heavy
industry, umbrellas, cranes, orange buses, beehives along the
road.

          "Mental open door limited by Party rigidity, karma of past
crimes, official figure 20,000,000 'bad elements' sent to work
camps country or killed 1957-1976. Merry Xmas Happy
Hanukah New York to Miriam & Didi--
          Allen Ginsberg."

The 'Zap stayed longer than the rest
   though he was dragged to bed for a couple of weeks
          with a ghastly flu
But, his vim always victorious,
          kept touring and teaching in China
till December 28
   when he returned to San Francisco

In China there was a flurry of interesting poems,
including a dream wherein
William Carlos Williams
dictated to him
a narrow-lined work
(published in *White Shroud* as
"Written in My Dream by W. C. Williams"

& "I Love Old Whitman So"
written in Baoding
after speed-reading through
*Leaves*
yet one more time.

•

While the bard was in China
there was some trouble in the Forest Ginsberg
when Peter went a bit crazy
on the Lower East Side again
He was drinking too much–
He showed up naked at 437 East 12th
with a machete
threatening to sever his own head

& was taken to Bellevue
tied to a chair

Allen & Peter were advised
by a psychiatrist
not to see each other for a year

Peter went to Chögyam Trungpa's center in Nova Scotia
& Karmê Chöling in VT

## 1985

In January
the photo show, called "Hideous Human Angels"
at the Holly Solomon Gallery
was a fiscal success
& another strollway opened wide
in the Forest Ginsberg

I count 47
photo shows
all o'er th' world
'tween '85 & '96

February 2
    Harper & Row published
        *Collected Poems 1947-1980*

    It was one of the best-selling books of verse
                    in the history of western civilization

& the reviews flowed forth–

    It upset Gary Snyder
    that the *Collected Poems*
            was snubbed by the official culture

    didn't get the awards it was due
    He mentioned the Pulitzer
            & the National Book Award

I could guess why
What Kenneth Rexroth called "The light from Plymouth Rock"
        still beams mightily
                o'er what used to be called squaresville–
        There were too many hard cocks
        trails of semen
                & attacks on the military-
        industrial surrealists

        to win corporate sponsorship

## HARRY SMITH: HOUSEGUEST

'85 was the year the artist/filmmaker/magician
Harry Smith
        came over to visit
–a car backed into him & fractured his knee–
he was homeless
& stayed about a year in the bard's guest room

"Harry Smith painter, filmmaker, sound archivist
& occult bibliophile, roommate for bulk of year"
                    is how the bard described it in
                    his biographic précis

The bard had always attracted the verbally combative
such as Kerouac, Lucien Carr, Barbara Rubin, Burroughs,
Corso–
            some of the sharpest tongues in a
                            sharp-tongued time
& now Harry
            One part of his brain a brilliant creator
One part a ruthless destroyer
                    capable of even gutting his own work
& a wit as pointy as a laser knife

It wore on Allen
            though one of his finest photographs
            (the first on his new large-neg Rolleiflex)
            had been taken of Harry not long before
                    in Harry's tiny room at the Breslin Hotel
                            pouring some milk.

When Bob Dylan came over for a visit
Harry refused to get up
            and chat with the singer.

Dylan (and much of his generation)
                            had been impacted by
Harry's famous Folkways collection
                    *Anthology of American Folk Music*

Allen's psychiatrist finally
suggested that
Harry had to depart
because he was raising the Ginzap's blood pressure

### SUMMER 1985
Naropa in Boulder

There was a symposium with William Burroughs & Norman Mailer
on the subject
            "The Soul: Is There One, What Is It, & What's Happening
                    to It?"

I recalled a dinner
        at Burroughs' bunker on the Bowery
                on Valentine's night '74:

He was talking about the Soul
how out-of-body sex was possible
like John Donne's
        floating lovers
& how he also believed that
souls crisp up and die
        at 10,000 degrees
& that was America's great sin:
it was the nation that first murdered souls.

•

November-December 1985 the bard went to Moscow
        with a writers' delegation
        from the American Academy of Arts & Letters
There's an eery snapshot by the bard of
writer Louis Auchincloss
        standing next to Dostoyevsky's writing desk
                at the Dostoyevsky Museum
                        in Leningrad
(in 'Zap's 1990 photo book from Twelvetrees Press)

It was just before Glasnost
and the bard complained of political and erotic censorship
whereupon a bureaucrat with the Moscow Writers Union said
        "Henry Miller will never be published in the Soviet Union."

## 1986

The bard became Distinguished Professor at Brooklyn College
replacing John Ashbery
        who was in the second year of
        his MacArthur Fellowship
Ashbery had invited Allen to B.C. a couple of times
& had been impressed with Allen's teaching at Naropa

        and so recommended him for the gig.

It was a good choice.
Ginsberg began at something like $60k
   (it advanced to $85k during
      his years there)

& later also taught at the CCNY graduate school
     on West 42nd

Freed from his administrative duties at Naropa
the bard tossed himself into his new gig
    with an überworkaholic dedication
–with the same
high metabolism, guilt & need for bardic laurels–
     –working too hard
     when sleep was required
     tired eyes like bruised apples–
   that he gave to his photos
   his diaries
    his politics
     his love life
      his search for verse

## THE NICARAGUA STATEMENT

At the PEN International Conference in NYC
he drafted, with Arthur Miller and Günter Grass
    what he called a
"controversial widely endorsed delegates'
statement against American
   intervention in Nicaragua"

and he went for the second time
to the Ruben Darío Poetry Festival
   in Nicaragua

   We have noted now & then on the bard's
   complex relationships with Cultures:

  Italy  England  France  Germany  Scandinavia
  Russia  Eastern Europe: Poland, Czech. & Hungary
  China  & of course India

In each place
        he had pals
            and passions

For instance, India
Indira Gandhi had been at the Royal Albert Hall in '65
                            when Ginsberg read
Also there was a woman named Pupil Jayakar,
                    a close friend of Gandhi's
Around 1985 A.G. was contacted
by Pupil Jayakar, then the Indian minister of culture
who wanted the bard to organize a poetry reading
as part of a two-year Festival of India

Allen accepted the task
but basically handed the project
                over to Bob Rosenthal

who recalled, "Allen suggested a pan-India festival with tribal
dancers, Vedic chanters, Baul poets Dallit (untouchable) poets"
            as well as several poet friends from Calcutta

This was under the umbrella of A.G.'s
                        Committee on Poetry

Part of it was a Festival of Poets in Bhopal
for which Rosenthal worked with the Indian gov't
"and got together a tour in the USA  which included bilingual
readings at the Museum of Modern Art in NYC hosted by Lita Hornick,
UCLA,  Santa Fe and maybe Chicago."

                Another example of
                the vast
                ◯     's of the 'Zap.

## 60 YEARS ON EARTH

            There was a
*Festschrift: Best Minds: A Tribute to Allen Ginsberg,*
        edited by Bill Morgan and Bob Rosenthal
                    with glory-zings from the likes of
                    Cage, Creeley & other best minds.

He wrote a foreword to John Wieners' *Selected Poems: 1958-1984*
                    for Black Sparrow Press

                                    •

          *White Shroud: Poems 1980-1985* out from
              Harper & Row

               with some of his finest verse
                         including the title poem

Out too that year the interesting
                    *Howl Annotated*
                         edited by Barry Miles
                              from Harper & Row
It was modeled on the *Waste Land* facsimile book
& featured scans of the original
               typed manuscript of Part I
                    with numerous hand corrections

          and then also facsimiles
               of four subsequent drafts
                         with their many alterations

          & then 18 typed drafts
          of Part II  ("What sphinx of cement & aluminum. . . .")

          & then various version of Part III
          ("Carl Solomon, I'm with you in Rockland")

          & also various versions of the "Footnote to Howl,"
          ("Holy!  Holy!  Holy!")
          some of which I thought were
                    a little better than the Footnote the
                              Bard finally chose

                                    •

     There was a "Howl" 30th anniversary panel
                    & Gala Reading at the MLA convention
                                   in NYC

## SUMMER OF 1986

A  man of means in Texas named Michael Minzer
wanted to finance a  CD project starring Ginsberg

He'd already produced a recording in Dallas
            of "Airplane Blues" and Blake's "Nurses Song"

Minzer met that summer with young Hal Willner
        who'd been music coordinator for NBC's "Saturday Night Live"
        since '81
        Willner was renowned for his "multi-artist tribute productions"
            and asked Hal to produce the Ginzap

Willner has a tendency, going into such a project,
                    to project a maddening vagueness
                            as to particulars & methodology
but he is famous in the music world
                    for knitting fine art from Chaos.

Allen was skeptical for months
        –he was as scorched as Samuel Beckett's toast from
            being burned down by Columbia Records
            & from all the offers
                    o'er the years
                        that had wound up as
                                dried foam
                            on the failure bucket.

## MACEDONIA

The 'Zap was invited to Lake Ohrid in Macedonia
to the Struga Festival
            to receive their annual award
                        a laurel wreath of gold
            (last awarded to W. H. Auden)

Steve Taylor composed his remarkable string quartet piece
                            to "White Shroud"
& it was premiered August 25 in a cathedral
                        with the Pro Arte Quartet
under the ikon painting of the black Madonna
            on the inside of the dome

On this tour the 'Zap also went to Budapest
& and also some benefits for Solidarity
                in Krakow & Warsaw

# PART XXIX

## 1987

Peter & Allen's year of planned separation ended
Peter wanted A.G. to sell his archives
                & move with Peter to
                Chögyam Trungpa's Buddhist center in Nova Scotia
                and bring there also Peter's sister, brothers & mother

Meanwhile Trungpa
                was gravely ill
                                He'd been in and out of a coma
                                for a number of months
                from too many Bacchus vines
                                on the Vajra

                                •

This was the year the Bard tried to
                                "slow down"
Of course perhaps his own metabolism
                was signaling the braking
He had now passed over the festschrift
                                year

Why are some writers so Driven?
I think of the frantic eyes
of Dickens & Dostoyevsky
                for instance

& Ginsberg
                "my queer shoulder at the wheel"

always groaning
o'er all the work
                that teemed on his desk

## APRIL 4

Trungpa passed away of heart failure on April 4

His body was embalmed in salt
and placed in a meditation position
   in an upright closed box of wood

at the Karmê Chöling center
   in the Green Mountains of Vermont

& carried in a procession
to a two-story brick stupa
  in a meadow
   and there atop it
    the leader was cremated

with thousands assembled.

The bard was once again seeing flames
   & smoke
    eat love.

"Universe is Person,"
   the bard once wrote.
"Mind is outer space,"
   he also wrote.
"Candor ends paranoia,"
   a sentence for the Path

## MAY 9
### BAD BLOOD

There was a three-day symposium
at St. Mark's Church
to mark the 20th Anniversary of the Poetry Project
   with readings and panels

I'd ended the reading on Saturday night
with my "Yiddish Speaking Socialists of the Lower East Side"
sliding my hands into the gloves of the Pulse Lyre
   to forge sweet tones
    beneath those socialist days

A bunch of us went out afterward to the Taj Restaurant
                              on East 6th
(Ed Dorn, Alice Notley, Ginsberg, Jerry Rothenberg,
Anselm Hollo, Bob Rosenthal, Anne Waldman
                              & others)


I was feeling upbeat rather than beat-up
I showed everybody the plastic handcuffs
I'd kept as a souvenir
            from the sit-in a few days before
                        at the CIA in Langley.


Allen sat across from me &
mentioned John Clellon Holmes
locked on the path of mouth cancer
how he'd had his jaw, his
tongue & part of his throat removed–
it will give him an extra year, he said,
to write more, & wind up
his affairs


    & then we were talking about
                cyclical vengeance
He said there was speculation that the MOSSAD was behind
the murders of Indira Gandhi & and Anwar el-Sadat
                        to block peace
(Gandhi had been at A.G.'s reading at Royal Albert Hall in '65)


He'd thought it was paranoia
            till he brought it up with William Burroughs
            who thought it not at all impossible


"It's a terrible problem," he said,
            "Bad blood"


& then the bard who was famous for being able to chant verse
                        by the hour
who knew poems like "Lycidas" by heart
then recited some lines
            from Yeats' "Meditations in Time of Civil War":

"'Vengeance upon the murderers,' the cry goes up,
'Vengeance for Jacques Molay.' In cloud-pale rages, or in lace,
The rage-driven, rage-tormented, and rage-hungry troop,
Trooper belaboring trooper, biting at arm or at face,
Plunges towards nothing, arms and fingers spreading wide
For the embrace of nothing; and I, my wits astray
Because of all that senseless tumult, all but cried
For vengeance on the murderers of Jacques Molay."

*Bad Blood  Bad Blood*
*Born in the Time-Flood*

## SUMMER OF '87

Allen was pulling his text-dappled oar
    on his teeming Boat of Books
        at the Naropa summer session

They had invited Marianne Faithfull to teach.
Her CD *Strange Weather*, produced by Hal Willner
    had just come out
        and it was impressive–

she had a thick-woven, true-toned voice
          you liked to hear.
Faithfull played her CD for the bard
& Allen gave her some cassettes of his tunes in exchange

She listened
    & then made a lawyerly pronouncement
          "Maybe you shouldn't sing"

The message was don't sing  please don't sing
    but you're a great reciter of
        your great American lines

That settled it.  Allen decided to work with Willner
on a spoken verse/music project
    in the hugely cool tradition of
        Kenneth Patchen, Kenneth Rexroth
        & the Kerouac/Steve Allen session

Allen went back to New York
              after the close of Naropa's season.

The bard, Willner, and exec. producer Minzer
chose 80 poems
              which A.G. read one night at his pad on East 12th

Everybody listened to the tapes
& the 80 was winnowed to 50.
Willner has very extensive contacts
                            among the better musicians and composers
He contacted about 12 of them &
invited them to A&R Studio in NYC to hear A.G. read his verse

A.G. rerecorded the selections for six hours, then
                            poems were assigned to composers such as
Gary Windo, Steve Swallow, Mark Bingham, Arto Lindsay,
              Marc Ribot, G.E. Smith, Lenny Pickett, Bill Frissell, et al.

They created music to swoop around the words
17 pieces
that flowed across the A.G. bardic passion-zone
from tender family memories to rougher modes
              –from "To Aunt Rose" to "Shrouded Stranger" to "Kral Majales"
                            to the spank-me ditty "C'mon Jack"

        After a week in the studio
        A.G. performed with some of the musicians
        at the Bottom Line in NYC
                    on August 21

        as part of a Fugs reunion
                    in honor of the 20th anniversary of the
                                        Summer of Love
              Peter Orlovsky was there.
              During one of our tunes
              he started screaming "Lydia! Lydia!"
              in a soprano voice
                            over and over
              enraging some of the audience
              & then security guys
                            carried him away
                                eyes widened
                            & legs spread wide

(The sessions and mixing for Allen's project
continued into the next year
—Chris Blackwell and Kim Buie of Island liked the project
      & voted to release *The Lion for Real*)

•

There was a festival inspired by the presence of
William Burroughs in Lawrence, Kansas
   in August of '87
     called the River City Reunion

A.G. had an exhibition of his photos at Lawrence
& gave a beautiful reading of
     "Howl"

Much of the audience could follow it
      with pursing lips
or memory-flashes
   as if listening
     to great music long familiar

Allen had suggested that Hal Willner
     produce a CD of Burroughs

so Willner visited Burroughs at his house
to begin the CD project known as *Dead City Radio*

Another project brought into place by the
     bard of howl.

•

There's a general bardic rule
    that says that a poet
     should never declare herself
      a deity

yet on October 31
A.G. tossed off a brief poem called "Proclamation"
which began
   *I am the King of the Universe*
   *I am the Messiah with a new dispensation*

It was the mindset of
      wanting to stroll naked through
      Cambridge in 1962
      after his first psilocybin with Leary

or, say, 1948, when he crawled out on
the fire escape in Harlem
      to startle the neighbors with
      "I've seen God!"

### PEACE NOW 1988

Early in the year called '88
he flew to Israel
to teach a course called Photographic Poetics
      with Robert Frank
      at the Camera Obscura School in Tel Aviv

      While there in Tel Aviv
      he took part in a huge Peace Now demonstration
against the bad treatment of Palestinians
in occupied territories

He read his 1974 poem "Jaweh & Allah Battle"
      before a crowd of 60,000
(one of his best political poems,
 ranking, say, with the 1980 eco-chant "Homework"
"Jaweh & Allah Battle" was
      later set by Philip Glass as part of *Hydrogen Jukebox*)

Back in New York
the bard began attending weekly meetings
with around 100 Jewish writers/artists
(among them, Norman Mailer, Kate Millett, Susan Sontag,
      Erica Jong, & Roy Lichtenstein)
      to forge a stand on the treatment of Palestinians

      A.G. arranged to have the PEN Center come out against
Israeli censorship of writers and newspapers

# PART XXX

## AN OPERA WITH GLASS

The opera *Hydrogen Jukebox* began calmly enough
when Philip Glass ran into A.G.
          in the St. Mark's Bookshop

and asked the bard if he'd perform with him
at a benefit for the Vietnam Veterans Theater
at the Schubert Theater

Allen took down from the store shelf
*The Fall of America*
        and showed Glass "Wichita Vortex Sutra"

    The performance went well
    and there were meetings at
    Ginsberg's apt to plan a grand collaboration

Work began in earnest in the fall of 1988
with neither Glass nor Ginzap
impressed with the
        wormwoody proposals of Dukakis or Reagan
        in the struggle for the Presidency

They selected a trail of verse
as a descant on the real America
        and its real future–
Did the bard chant accurately
        when he named one of his books
        *The Fall of America?*

Glass and Ginsberg selected sections & slivers
"Iron Horse," the beautiful "To Aunt Rose"
      Peter O's 29th birthday poem from Calcutta '62,
        "Wichita Vortex Sutra"
"Going to Chicago"
    "The Green Automobile"
        "Cabin in the Woods"

and the 1974
"Jahweh and Allah Battle"
        fresh in mind from chanting it in Tel Aviv,

the Moloch section of "Howl"
    "The Green Automobile,"
& sections from the "National Security Agency Dope Calypso"
                    intermingled with his poem "Violence"

& ending with the
        po/tune he composed on the plane
        coming back from Boulder after father Louis passed:
                            "Father Death Blues"

    (The American Music Theater in Philadelphia
                sponsored perf's in the spring of 1990
    w/ the world premieres at the Spoleto Festival in Charleston,
    SC & Spoleto, Italy in June 1990)

    The opera featured six singers, a small ensemble of keys,
    winds & percussion, with Martin Goldray directing

                            •

In '88 there was another opera
            based on the bard's works
at th' Hamburg State Opera House
titled "Cosmopolitan Greetings"
        with Robert Wilson directing & music by George Gruntz

                            •

    A tour of Japan next
    with readings,
        plus an antinuke rally in Osaka

    & benefits at Seika & Kyoto Universities
    with his friend the poet Nanao Sakaki
        "to protect Okanawan Shiraho Blue Coral Reef."

### JUNE 25, 1988

    Lowell, Massachusetts began to
    celebrate its hometown boy
                    Jack Kerouac

    In late June they dedicated the
    Kerouac Commemorative Park

with 15 passages from Kerouac
cut upon 8 three-sided granite columns
more or less dolmen'd
into the array of a mandala

## HARRY SMITH

Harry could be like a lasery sandbur
        but had a gentle fraction inside
                        that brought him intense friendships
                especially with women

Miriam would talk with Harry for hours on the phone
                                over the years
so A.G. arranged for Harry
                to live at Naropa as a kind of
                        "Shaman-in-Residence"
He had a cottage on campus
        which became a kind of Seekers' Abode
                                an Adytum
        where he collected things, made hundreds of tape recordings
        from '88 to '91

                (After Harry passed away it
                became the Naropa hand-set print shop.

—A.G. had first met Harry in the '50s at the Five Spot
at a Thelonius Monk gig. Harry was taking notes on
Monk's syncopation. Harry brought Allen to his pad
and rolled some of his movies. Later A.G. took a reel
to Jonas Mekas, thus introducing Harry
                to the prime instigator of the
                underground movie movement)

                        •

The 'Zap delivered
the Charles Olson Memorial lectures
                        at SUNY Buffalo

Meanwhile his photo career was in full careen, with
shows in Tokyo, Krakow, Warsaw, Tübingen, Whistler House in Lowell,
Fogg Museum in Cambridge, Vision Gallery in Boston, & Tilton Gallery
in NYC

•

The end of the century saw the
> kudzuing of ghastly right-wing think tanks
> & foundations
> > well funded & weird

In October o' '88
the right-winger's right-winger, Senator Jesse Helms,
with the help of the Heritage Foundation
vom'd forth a law which forced the FCC
to enforce a 24-hour ban on "indecent" language
> > on all the nation's airwaves

The 'Zap realized "There goes 'Howl'"
& so, again, rose to the protection

& in his own words "organized consortium P.E.N. American Center.
A.C.L.U. with Pacifica Radio to oppose FCC censorship of arts broad-
casting."

(The results? There were court decisions in 1993 which left in
place a ban on erotolalia from 6 A.M. to 8 P.M., with freedom to
chant eros over the air from late in the evening till dawn.)

### POE JOB PHOBIA

> I spoke with the bard  on 12-16-88
> He was in the hospital
> He seemed short of breath
> The dr., he said, told him
> > he was healing like a young man
> I was calling to ask him to
> perform at place called the Kitchen in January
> to protest the crackdown in Czechoslovakia
> > on the Plastic People band
> > and a cultural leader named
> > > Ivan Jirous

> He said, "If I'm healthy, count me in."

He said he'd been reading a hostile biography of Bob Dylan
& we talked a bit about what I'd come to call the "Poe Job"

such as what Goldman had done to Lennon
The Poe Job of course goes all the way back to
Rev. Rufus Griswold's hate-bio of the Raven man

The bard was feeling a bit Poe'd himself
He'd read the manuscript of Barry Miles' biography
      which was about to come out
and he felt Miles was harsh on his Buddhism
by which I guess he meant
   the considerable space
   Miles devoted to
      the '75 stripping at Snowmass
      & its literary aftermath.

## 1989

We gathered January 29 at the perf space called the Kitchen
        on West 19th
to call upon the government of Czechoslovakia
    to give total freedom of speech
    to its artists and singers

There were many performers, including Eliot Sharp,
Vicki Stanbury & the Plastic People's own
    Bratlislav Brabenec
    with his long-toned saxophone

Allen had healed enough to
    read "Kral Majales"

and Steve Taylor & I sang my
"Incantation Against the Government of Czechoslovakia"

to the overflow crowd.

Not many months ahead:
    the nonviolent rev in Czechoslovakia

•

The 'Zap was honored at a banquet February 11
at the Associated Writing Program's Convention
      in Philadelphia

The Fugs performed with the bard.
We wrote a melody to
his '55 masterwork
          "The weight of the world is love."

& it still gives a thrill to listen to the tape of it
from that night
          with 1,000 screaming writers & professors
          at its close

At the end A.G. and the Fugs sang Blake's "Nurse's Song"
with the sing-along final lines,
          repeated o'er and o'er
          "& All the Hills Echoéd"
          to an ecstatic crooning auditorium

again a thrill to hear
          over 10 years later
Allen's voice had all its fine bass qualities
that night
          in key     in control     & reaching
                         his golden thread toward Blake

                    •

Barry Miles' 533 page biography *Ginsberg*
          was published by Simon & Schuster

          I liked its honesty
          & how Miles was able
                    close as he was to the bard
               to get to a critical distance

                    •

          As for Allen, there was a further frenzy
          of readings at schools & colleges
          He kept up the flow of fund-raisers
          that  year
                    I count at least 11 benefits

for WNYC, AIDS Prevention, Abbie Hoffman
Foundation, Lower East Side homesteaders, squatters,
Hanuman Books, Albert Hoffman Memorial Library in LA,
                                             et alia

In addition he had some more photo exhibitions
                in LA, Chi, Poland, Austria & Germany

and his fine spoken verse/music CD
*The Lion for Real*
        by Great Jones/Island Records
        produced by Hal Willner
        (secret executive producer  Michael Minzer)

•

In May he moved his office from his East 12th pad
to 2nd Avenue & 14th
        subletting two rooms from the daughter
        of Arlene Lee
(Lucien Carr's ex & Mardou Fox in K.'s *Subterraneans*. It was in torrid
eros with Arlene Lee in the '50s, A.G. once told me,
          that his dong was perma-bent to the left)

Then a few months later
the office moved to 41 Union Square, th' 14th floor

        probably the only poet
        ever to have his own staff
        & office in the former Great Zone
                of the Left

•

In a more controversial area
he attended a NAMBLA convention in '89

Sometimes he complained to me he was being attacked
from the right for his love of youth

He was always extremely candid in matters of eros
"Candor ends paranoia"
        he wrote in "Cosmopolitan Greetings"
but he would travel to colleges
        & give forth the message
        it was okay to make it with
            his legal-age students

& now and then I give a reading at a college

where they still talk of the furor from
                                        A.G. erotic talk
                                                    of decades ago

"I myself don't
like underage boys," he once told *The New York Times*
'But they have a right
to talk about the
                    age of consent.
I see it as a free speech issue–
a discussion of the law."

                            •

The bard helped get a three-year grant
                        for Harry Smith
                from the Grateful Dead's Rex Foundation

On December 2, Bush & Gorbachev
announced the end of the Cold War

                        and on December 29
                        the writer Vaclav Havel
                        was elected the president of Czechoslovakia

## PART XXXI

### 1990

In March A.G. came to the Zen Center
                                    near Woodstock
with Anne Waldman.
He recited the libretto of *Hydrogen Jukebox*

Later we chatted
He told me that Burroughs
            sold $180k of his shotgun-paint-tube-splatter
            on-plywood/collage paintings last year
He'd taken up art after his trilogy
            *Cities of the Red Night*
                *The Place of Dead Roads*
                    & *The Western Lands*

Burroughs gets up, Allen said, smokes a j
takes his methadone,
writes till 4 P.M.
            then dinner & a few drinks, then zzz

"And he's healthy!"
            the bard said with a cackle,
comparing W.B. to himself
crunched with high blood pressure,
                        gout, diabetes, et al.

## PRAGUE

That spring Allen organized a visit to Prague
        to celebrate the warless revolution

He'd not been back since
            being tossed in '65

This time he was received by the Lord Mayor Mr. Koran
& President Vaclav Havel

and re-laureled as King of the May once again!
and toured various colleges
            reading & lecturing

                    •

*Hydrogen Jukebox* premiered
                with Philip Glass
at the Spoleto Festivals
                in Charleston, SC & Spoleto, Italy

I spoke with him when he returned
& he mentioned how he dug being called Maestro
                        at opera houses

                    •

The 'Zap was an American delegate
            to the 12th World Congress of Poets
                    in Seoul, SK

& out came the large-format book
by Twelvetrees Press called
        *Allen Ginsberg Photographs*

And what was probably the first lecture by a major poet
in the history of Western civilization:
"Chemical Substances & Poetics,"
at the School of Pharmacy
at SUNY, Albany

## A GOOD SYSTEM FOR BARDING AROUND

In his final years
the bard had the same stage setup
wherever he read

A sketch of the stage was included in a rider
to his contracts:

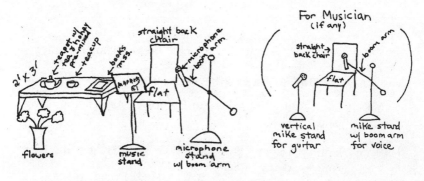

The flowers on the lower left were to be,
in the bard's words, "a modest bunch of flowers, preferably
non-florist, local weeds or garden growth."

His rider also called for a pot of chamomile tea and honey
"already pre-mixed to save mess of honey on mss. and audience time."

## 1991

Around the time of the Gulf War's
inception of spent uranium-shell bombardment

Ginzap was a guest lecturer for a week
at the Virginia Military Institute

There's a fine photo by Gordon Ball
showing cadets in grey uniforms
              reading "Howl"
                        one with his long thin fingers
                        wrapped up over his short-shorn hair

Oddly it was America's poets who sensed
              the underlying
              sham of Desert Storm
& Allen joined Poets Against the Gulf War

•

There was a MLA Special Session on "Kaddish"
with Gordon Ball and Helen Vendler
              in San Francisco

and the book *Allen Ginsberg Photographs*
              from Twelvetrees Press in Santa Monica

## MORE SCURRY HURRY FLURRY OF '91

•Master Class at the Walt Whitman Birthplace Association, Long
    Island, NY

•Symposium on Tiananmen Square with Feng Lizhi at the New
    York Academy of Sciences

•Keynote Speaker, Buddhist Psychology Conference, at th' Karma
    Triyana Monastery in Woodstock, NY

•Symposium with Lewis Hyde, "Art & Politics," at Kenyon College,
    Ohio

•Great Falls Preservation and Development Corporation 200th
    Anniversary, Paterson, NJ

•Reading Jack Kerouac's *Dharma Bums* & Jacob Rabinowitz's
    *Translations of Catullus* for Spring Audio Cassettes, NY

•Harriet Monroe Poetry Award at the University of Chicago

## TOUCHING THE COOLING NOGGIN

November 27, '91
Harry Smith died at the Chelsea Hotel

The bard heard about it & rushed to the hospital
Harry had been coughing blood,
and finally it was copious,
   & he was found in his room.
They tried to revive him, a crew from Saint Vincents,
but he was gone.
Allen thinks he came back from Boulder
       to N.Y. to die.
A.G. went into the hospital morgue
& sat with him.  One eye was semi-open, he told me,
& the other bruised from the fall.
There was a tube still in his mouth,
a bandage keeping it there, & blood
on his beard.  His head hair was white
& fine– Allen felt it--the head was
still warm.
He meditated, he said, for an hour-- a Tibetan
tradition apparently.
   Later there was a memorial at St. Mark's Church
   at which Harry's friends, and the Fugs,
     sang & eulogized him,
     and also Harry's branch of the
      Ordo Templi Orientis
       performed a Gnostic Mass
       for the departed artist

      •

Tuli Kupferberg told me at the end of December
that A.G. was in the hospital in Cooperstown
with liver problems.
Perhaps the hepatitis C
   that was to eat his life
     five years later.

## 1992

The bard with the legendary vim
always bounded back
                    from his illnesses
There was a party for the *Portable Beat Reader*
at the Poetry Project at St. Mark's Church
                    February 5


Joyce Johnson, Hettie Jones, Ann Charters, Peter O.,
Herbert Huncke, Allen and I read


It was a fine, unsentimental evening
& afterwards Miriam & I, Ann Charters & A.G.
had a late dinner at
                    Kiev on 2nd Ave. & 7th.


He mentioned how he had helped Jan Kerouac
sue for a share in Jack's estate
                    She now got 50%, he said.


                    •


In Paris the French minister of culture, Jacques Lang
presented the bard with the
Chevalier de l'Ordre des Artes et des Lettres


          & he was also elected
          fellow of the American Academy of Arts & Sciences
                              in Boston

### NODDING AT NAROPA

I taught a course at Naropa that summer
on setting up multi-decade information systems
                    to assist in the long-term writing of verse.
Our apartment
          was next to A.G.'s


which gave us the first evidence
                    of the bard's declining health

I was distressed at his condition
He could be seen sleeping at readings
He had severe diabetes
& at dinner parties
> he would excuse himself
>> to rush back to his apt
>>> to shoot up his insulin

& was restricted to a stringent macrobiotic diet

> yet noddy as he seemed
> his legendary metabolism
>> kept foaming through
> to give us a sense
>> "This Bard is Forever."

•

That October
Michael Schumacher's 769 page
> biography of Ginsberg, called *Dharma Lion*
was published by St. Martin's Press

(*Dharma Lion*, read in conjunction with
Barry Miles' *Ginsberg*
> together give a hologrammatic
> view of the bard
>> from birth up into the late 1980s)

•

Brooklyn College
& CUNY Graduate Center:
> Walt Whitman centenary celebrations

(For a brilliant Ginsberg presentation on Whitman
read his essay, "Taking a Walk Through *Leaves of Grass*"
in A.G.'s *Deliberate Prose, Selected Essays*
> from HarperCollins, 2000

# PART XXXII

## 1993

A newspaper Long Island *Newsday*
asked the bard to compose a poem for
                    the upcoming occasion
                    of Bill Clinton's inauguration

so, after consulting friends, the bard put together his
        "New Democracy Wish List" on January 17

                    perhaps as a kind of response to Maya Angelou's
                    poem at the inauguration

It had many good points
                which Clinton mostly ignored
            (the bard sent him a copy)

                        •

February 28
the bard called with the ghastly word
that Carl Solomon
            had passed away that morning
                            from lung cancer

                        •

& a few days later, March 2
the World Trade Center bombing
                –fundamentalism cursing the American city

                        •

            March 26 I went to his apartment
            and filmed the bard reading his
                        "New Democracy Wish List"

            It was a fine slice of his '93 life
            because while we were running tape
            various pals called the bard,
            Phil Whalen, Gary Snyder,
                        and ex-governor Jerry Brown
                    who wanted A.G. to write a pamphlet
                            for a series he was starting

•

Around this time he began Buddhist retreats
with (and benefits for)
Gelek Rinpoche of
           Jewel Heart in Ann Arbor

plus annual benefits for Tibet House
    with Laurie Anderson
      & Philip Glass

•

The bard went to his 50th high school class reunion
           at Eastside H.S. in NJ

## SOLOMON

"ah Carl . . . now you're really in the total animal soup of time—"
         "Howl"

I always admired Solomon's
good-hearted, very aware Lonerism
& I was surprised
that no one seemed to be giving him a public memorial
to I called Ed Friedman at the St. Mark's Church
and Allen too of course

and helped organize the one
which was held at the church on June 16

    That day I bused to NYC from Woodstock
    and visited Allen's office on Union Square

    He had just come from a dr.'s appointment
    I was surprised at how much of the office was devoted
    to his photos!   There was a shot of a very beautiful
    Joanne Kyger from 1963
           & a young Harry Smith that looked
           just a tad like
               d. a. levy of Cleveland.

The bard gave me a big piece of kombu energy seaweed–
very expensive, he said, from a rich friend
He cracked off about a square foot–you chew it
    for proper bardic metabolism
Also a copy of Louis Ginsberg's collected works
& Solomon's final big book

The bard through the 33 years of crossed paths
always loaded me down with books, CDs,
    clippings, manifestoes & urgings

The highlight for me at the Solomon memorial
was singing harmony with Allen on the
   *Prajnaparamita sutra*
    while playing my 3-stringed Strum Stick

Ted Morgan, Ann Charters & others spoke
then Gregory Corso
read a fresh poem written in big scrawls
    on a crumpled & folded paper.

The bard closed the night with "Howl"
He started slowly, then built it up in a
    rhapsodic, rapturous way
He later said he'd given it an "operatic rendition."

Allen had to split almost at once
because he'd promised to appear that night
    at the opening of a club called Shaman.

•

That fall the 'Zap had a sabbatical from Brooklyn College
so in a *horror vacui temporis*
  he filled in the gap
  with a four-month tour of Europe

I saw him on September 5
    just before he left
He had come to Woodstock for my musical drama *Cassandra*

He'd read a pamphlet on Bosnia by George Soros, the financier
who was spending some of his millions
             promoting free trade & democracy
             in Eastern Europe

Soros was alarmed at the rise of nationalism
"His point," the bard said, "is that replacing the
Cold War mentality now
             is a hypernationalism
                      that threatens the peace
not only of Europe
             but of the whole world
             and that's going to be the big plague of the future
             and the cause of wars."

He taught with Anne Waldman at the interesting
Schule für Dichtung in Vienna in September

and went to Budapest, Belgrade, Bydgoszcz, Krakow,
                                      Lodz & Warsaw

Then traveled to premieres of
Jerry Aronson's *The Life and Times of Allen Ginsberg*
             in Paris, Berlin, Prague, Barcelona, Madrid, Córdoba
             and Athens
                      in a long ego-ribboning
                               line of praise & money-scoop

He performed in Berlin at a Jewish festival
& did a few tunes with the klezmer band, the Klezmatics.

In Athens he wrote one of his better hortatory poems
"C'mon Pigs of Western Civilization Eat More Grease"
             (in his final book *Death & Fame*)

He toured to Dublin
where he did what he called a "TV collaboration"
             with a rock star named Bono
                      of the band called U2

At trek's end the bard visited Paul Bowles in Tangiers
& the spots
> he had haunted with Peter Orlovsky
> & Jack Kerouac
>> back in '57 & '61

Then it was back to the States in January
> for a Vajrayogini Buddhist retreat with
Gelek Rinpoche in Michigan.
Gelek Rinpoche was Allen's Buddhist mentor
following the demise of Chögyam Trungpa.

•

*Hydrogen Jukebox*
which had been recorded in a studio in '92 and '93
was released as a CD by Elektra/Nonesuch

## 1994

The CD *Kronos Quartet* ★ *Howl USA*
>> came out early in the year
On it the bard performed the poem to music
on a CD that contained a piece called "Cold War Suite"
> with the voice of the great I. F. Stone!
On January 20 he performed "Howl" with the Quartet
>> at Carnegie Hall
*Tikkun* magazine honored
A.G. at its January 16-17 conference
> "because of his important contribution
> to progressive culture, and because of his unique
> blending of Jewish particularism & universalism."

## NEW AMAZING GRACE

Since '92 I'd been collecting verses
from poets & composers
> for *The New Amazing Grace*

The verses could be on any subject
and very secular
> except that I wanted just a faint beam of
> hope– like the "sunlight in the window"
>> in Naomi's final letter
>>> in "Kaddish"

NPR had picked up my quest and had broadcast a piece
on it
        so that a big influx of submissions had come in from
        ministers in the heartland & regular folk, but

I was having trouble getting *New Amazing Grace* verses
from some of my bards
Pete Seeger was one of them
Finally I wrote him to the effect that I couldn't
believe that one of the greatest songwriters
The guy who wrote "Turn, Turn, Turn,"
        & "Where Have All the Flowers Gone"
                & half of "If I Had a Hammer"

couldn't come up with
        a 4-line quatrain for *NAG.*

It worked.  Seeger finally mailed his in on April 14

Burroughs, Ferlinghetti and Ginsberg were other holdouts
though all ultimately came through

Allen called one evening in late January & said he had a verse
and started singing it.
        It was something like,
        "When you grow old
                you'll shit your pants . . ."

I broke in, "No! No!"
I never would have thought I'd ever edit or censor
                        my hero
but I mentioned that the NPR piece
had brought in a rinse of submissions
                from Methodist ministers
                & the regular folk of radio land

(I had no idea he was having incontinence problems
                        from his diabetes)

On March 14 he wrote:

"Re Amazing Grace– I've just
not been able to do anything– or
nothing's occurred to me– my head full
of panic at unfinished CD Rhino notes now
delaying release of the 4 CD's another
2 months, my overload responsible–
     I'll still try–
        Love Allen"
I wasn't sure he even knew the melody and meter for
           "Amazing Grace"
so I sent him a note with the
      metrical structure:

$$\cup - \cup - \cup - \cup -$$
$$\cup - \cup - \cup -$$
$$\cup - \cup - \cup - \cup -$$
$$\cup - \cup - \cup -$$

         in 3/4 time

Two weeks later he called
complaining that he'd been up all night

and sang me some very beautiful verses

After he'd finished
     & I'd remarked how excellent they were, he asked
"Do you know where I am now?"

"No."

"I'm on the toilet."

The verses arrived
    in the mail
       a few days later:

Stanzas for Amazing Grace

O homeless hand on many a street
Accept this change from me
A friendly smile or word is sweet
As fearless charity

Woe workingman who hears the cry
And cannot spare a dime
Nor look into a homeless eye
Afraid to give the time

So rich or poor no gold to talk
A smile on your face
The homeless poor where you may walk
Recieve amazing grace

I dreamed I dwelled in a homeless place
Where I was lost alone
Folk looked right through me into space
And passed with eyes of stone

Allen Ginsberg
4/21/94

with a note:

"Your last letter with ballad
meter ( ∨–∪–∪–∪– ), helped clarify the
form.

Here's 4 stanzas. The last
stanza could go first

Use 2, 3 or 4 of the stanzas
in any order you edit.

Thanks for the prompting &
persistence– but I lost a night's
sleep working it over!
                Love
                  Allen"

It was some of his
    final finest verse.

## MAY 8, 1994

I went to NYC to MC a panel at St. Mark's
                on Investigative Poetry
& once downtown I
called A.G.  He was just getting up
    after a party he'd thrown last night
            for his Brooklyn College students

He'd been dreaming, he said,
as he awakened, about Olson's poem
that begins "Mud & wattles" (#4 of "The Songs of Maximus")

He dubbed for me a tape of Joyce reading from
          *Finnegan's Wake*
and Wilde reading "Ballad of the Reading Gaol."

Then we went to the church
for the panel with Bernadette Mayer, Nourbese Philip,
David Henderson and A.G.

Then oodles of kids and poets to Ginsberg's for dinner,
then back to the church for a poetry reading
Backstage Allen told me that
    Jan Kerouac was going to hold a press conference
    at the upcoming NYU Beat Festival
        challenging Kerouac's mom's will
A slice of a day in
    the life of Allen

## MAY 15, 1994

I spoke with the 'Zap
He told me that Johnny Depp
had paid Kerouac's estate $50,000
for one of Jack's jackets
(I must have misheard him,
because I think it was only a mere $15,000)

## MAY 17-22, 1994
## NYU BEAT FEST

Its formal name was "The Beat Generation
                    Legacy and Celebration"

It was the kind of conference
            that the bard always
                    joyed to serve

in that it validated
            all the frenzied years
                    of forging a generation

It was sponsored by the NYU School of Ed
Ann Charters and A.G. were the honorary chairs

•

One of the B.G. panels was titled
"The Legacy, Connections & Influences"
with myself, Doug Brinkley, Gordon Ball and others.

I was innocently sitting at the red-clothed dais
when Hunter Thompson arrived
                    in a curl-brimmed beige campaign hat
                    & a green shirt
and handed me a lit hash pipe
            in front of 8 or 900 people
            in packed Eisner & Lubin Auditorium

What could I do but
            flow some smoke
                    from my distinguished writer pal?

•

They invited Jan Kerouac
who chanted some work
            at Eisner & Lubin Auditorium one evening

She was screwed-up physically at 42
Was on dialysis I heard

& yet she read with great vitality
     & even chant-sang a poem
          to a rap track

and looked not that different from when she
was a 14 year old wild child on Avenue B
          in 1966.

## MAY 19

There was a big reading at Town Hall on 43rd Street
of the poets at the conference

Anne Waldman & I MC'd
We called William Burroughs in
     Lawrence from a phone on the stage
          & he read a piece

Then later backstage
     based on what A.G. had told me
          I mentioned to Michael McClure
          that Johnny Depp
          had paid 50 grand
          to Kerouac's estate
          for one of
               Jack's jackets

     Ferlinghetti was out on the mike
          beauty-voweling his final poem

     Corso & the Russian poet Andrei Voznesensky
     were chatting nearby
     Ray Manzarek & McClure were just
               about to go out
          to do their poems w/ piano

     when McClure flipped me
     his hard-analysis Dorian eye, & said
          "I have five or six of those."

          "So do I," I replied,
           my mind shifting cunningly
          from free will
               to Goodwill

> thinking, of course, that
> Depp might need a
> 2nd coat for when
> the 1st is in the cleaners
> > & a third for his summer home

## A HOME FOR HIS ARCHIVES

Allen wanted his archives
> to go to his alma mater

but the Atropos/Lachesis/Clotho trinity
had other plans

The archives had been brought to a sense of order
after years of work by Bill Morgan
> (& also Jacqueline Gens)

A few years previously it had been appraised
in an item-by-item manner
> by Bob Wilson of the Phoenix Bookshop

at over $4 million
(and Bill Morgan told me Wilson
did not actually get through all the items)

It was a perilously lofty figure
> even for Irwin Allen Ginsberg.

In the end Columbia could not find the
> resources to acquire the trove

It turned out that Stanford University
had money–there had been a hiring freeze on personnel
The library wanted to spend their $
> on one large expensive item.

A scholar named Steve Watson
was doing some research at Stanford
The librarians there thought Columbia
> owned Allen's files
and when they were told otherwise
they called Bill Morgan

By now the bard had selected an unwobbling price
—a million dollars
(excluding A.G.'s massive photo archives)

Morgan negotiated back and forth for several weeks
with the bard's agent Andrew Wylie
            handling some of the fine points

among which was the provision that the bard
would be given 2 week's free room & board
            per year at Stanford
                  to visit his treasures

Key professors at Stanford, Marjorie Perloff in particular,
plus Gilbert Sorrentino and Diane Middlebrook
            stepped forth to urge the purchase.

# PART XXXIII

## A CELEBRATION OF THE BARD AT NAROPA

They organized a celebration
            of Allen that July at Naropa called
"Beats & Other Rebel Angels: A Tribute to Allen Ginsberg"
It was a huge one
& since there was a kind of
edge-of-frenzy
tap tap-ing at the edge of the Beat Generation anyway
there was Cannes-esque
            flavor to the celebration

as Meredith Monk, Miguel Algarin, Joanne Kyger, Ferlinghetti,
Amiri Baraka, Galway Kinnell, Sharon Olds, Robert Creeley,
Gregory Corso, Philip Glass, Michael McClure, Francesco Clemente,
Raymond Foye, Anne Waldman, David Cope, Gary Snyder, Antler,
Andy Clausen, Ken Kesey
            & a pleth' of Others
                  flew to the high air of Boulder.

They dedicated the Allen Ginsberg Library
                  July 3

My part included a lecture on July 5,
"The Ginsberg Method: How to Keep from Getting
Boxed-In in a Chaotic World."

## 7-8-94

I watched the great bard
        read his "Sunflower Sutra"

& jotted in my notebook,

        "How afire
        this spire"

•

There were a series of national ads for the Gap clothing line
One featured Andy Warhol, another William Burroughs
and one with the text:
        "Allen Ginsberg wore khakis"
for which the bard received $20,000
                which he donated to Naropa

He insisted that the ad state the Naropa donation
but it was printed in such small pointed type
                        that you needed a
                        magnifier to see it.

•

The bard did a book signing at Barnes & Noble in SF
which miffed Lawrence Ferlinghetti
                because of the store-eating
                        aspect of big chains.

Out came, in the fall o' '94,
the 4-CD set from Rhino Records called
*Holy Soul Jelly Roll  Poems & Songs 1949-1993*

& the 'Zap went forth on what they often call
        a "whirlwind" tour
                of signings & readings
                        to promote sales

## ARRIVALS AT STANFORD

In September o' '94
The bard's papers began arriving at Stanford

174,601 items in around 500 boxes
                all meticulously indexed w/

24,179 pp. of manuscripts
18.9k of "Journals & Notebooks"
                & 2,500 tape recordings

Hey o bright scribe of 2002,
want to write a 50,000-page
                bio of a bard?

                        •

The fall of '94 saw a right-winger named Newt Gingrich
& a ghastly cohort of like-minded wing nuts
                take over Congress
                for the first time in 40 years
the Senate too fell to a form of right-winger
                a bit more polite than Gingrich' sneer squad.

        The bard had a fearful take
        on the right-wingers froth-fingering
                        the throat of America
        They boded no good
                he felt
                for freedom,
                        especially for gays

and any who might fall into
the remarkable category of
                "madman beat in time"

## NEW AMAZING GRACE

I was barding around
        & flew to New York from Milwaukee
then headed to Allen's house on November 20
to get ready for the first performance
of the New Amazing Grace
a benefit for the Poetry Project & St. Mark's Church

We practiced at the church during the day
–a remarkable gathering of top-rank gospel singers
plus musicians such
            as Steve Taylor & Coby Batty

The audience was treated to a thrilling
                hour and a half
                of beautiful singing

The quatrains of Waldman, Rothenberg, Creeley,
Schickele, Seeger, Bly, Wakoski, Eshleman,
            and about 75 others
            soared to a sacred/secular zone
                        of great power

But it was when Allen Ginsberg walked upon the
stage among the singers
            to soft-voice his four amazing quatrains
        that the summit was found

The audience had been given copies of all the lyrics
        and encouraged to sing along.
        By the close of the evening
        everyone was on their feet and trembling the walls

### 1995

There were at least 3 trips to Europe
                    that year
& at least 8 benefits
        plus oodles of gigs in the States.

•

    For five days in May '95
    he read all the poems in his upcoming
    *Selected Poems: 1947-1995*
            at the Knitting Factory on Leonard Street.
            8 P.M. show time, $16

    The five gigs were video'd with a 3-camera shoot

•

June 1, he suffered a pulmonary embolism
an obstruction of the lung
    by an embolus, any foreign substance
    such as a blood clot or dislodged tumor cells
    It's
a very serious condition that usually requires
   at least a few days in the hospital

yet somehow the bard found vim enough for a conference called
   "The Writings of Jack Kerouac"
     at NYU  on June 4, 5 & 6

Panels had names such as "Bop, Blues and Scat: the Jazz Nexus
   in Kerouac's Writing"

    & "Language, Voice, Beat and Energy of
    Kerouac's Poetry"

The latter panel was chaired by Allen G
on the morning of June 5
    at NYU's Eisner & Lubin Auditorium

Just before it began
Jan Kerouac approached the bard and asked to
make a brief announcement that the NY Public Library
   & the Bancroft Library at the U of Cal
   had offered $1 million for
      her father's archives

She was not allowed
   There were some exasperated words
& apparently security guards escorted her out

Meanwhile a long banner was unfurled in the room
    "SAVE JACK'S PAPERS"

•

A group of poets calling themselves the Unbearables
held some parody events
–such as a Kerouac Impersonator contest–
   calling the $120 per head NYU conference
   "The Beats Sell Out"

June 6 was a big night at Town Hall
            on 43rd Street off 6th Avenue called
"An Evening With Jack Kerouac: Poetry and Prose with Music"

            As I entered the Unbearables picket line was chanting
            "Where are the Fugs
            Now that we need them?"

A bunch of us read, focusing on Kerouac's writing
Graham Parker, Odetta, Anne Waldman, myself, & others
including Gregory Corso
            who wowed them
            by complying when the audience
            shouted for "Marriage"

Annie Leibovitz was posing us
for *Vanity Fair*
            in the upstairs dressing room at Town Hall

I sat next to Allen
            who looked weak and sallow

He said he'd had a pulmonary embolism last week
They'd done a chest X ray
and it had blipped on the negative

How big? I asked
About the size of a Spanish olive,
                        he replied.

It went away, he said, with medication
He seemed trembly
            & couldn't stand
                        for a long time

Then how come
            you're going to Italy tomorrow?
                        I asked
He said his schedule was light
and then he'd have 9 days to heal at Francesco Clemente's place
in Amalfi in the south near Naples
            before returning to his summer duties

I held his hand
           & marveled once again at his power.

Then we were standing offstage
by gilt-wood sconces
                topped with stylized artichokes

Allen was getting ready to be driven home
to rest for his flight
              to his photo exhibit at the Venice Biennale

I was seeing the Rot Bird
          as Graham Parker and Odetta
                  read Kerouac's prose

O Rot Bird I see your beak-bites
              in the gilt-wood sconces
        on the backstage wall
        where the bard stands
                next to the boxes of mike stands

"You *have* to live as long as your daddy,"
              I said to him
"I will," he replied

but I could hear the
          wings of the Rot Bird
              whirring in the nerves
                  of Kerouac's words
                      as Allen exited stage right
                            to his cab.

•

The 'Zap made it to his photo exhibit "108 Images" at
                the Venice Biennale on June 8
with Hiro Yamagata, a rich & famous Japanese artist
who was reported to be supporting Gregory Corso
                with $3,500 a month
The invitation to the Yamagata Venice exhibition
bore a color photo of a psychedelically painted
Rolls Royce convertible
              with whitewalls
                  parked in an opulent yard

•

With the money from the
            Stanford archives purchase
A.G. purchased and rehabbed
Claes Oldenburg's former loft
            on East 13th near 1st Avenue
            Larry Rivers also lived in the building

(Oddly enough they found the place
in an ad in the *Times*.
Rosenthal hired an architect
though the bard worked on the design
& the long loft was completely redone,
            with separate offices & a guest room)

Allen told me that the monthly maintenance
was kept low
            because a McDonalds
            rented the ground floor
                        on the 14th Street side of the
                                    building

There was a bit of jeering and sneering in the media
over the sale of his archives.

In an interview with *The New York Times*
he said that his agent got 5%, the archivist Bill Morgan
who slaved 13 years on the trove
            & set up the deal 10%
plus a giant slice for taxes &
            "I was left with a third
            I bought the loft
            Now I'm back to square one."

All of us wanted him to get into
that building as quickly as possible

One night Miriam and I walked the bard
up the three flights to his apartment on E. 12th
& it was a painful experience

He walked very very slowly
pausing at each landing
                    breathing heavily

I was reminded of how Chekhov
in his final winter
              decided to stay in Moscow
                      to be with his wife Olga Knipper
but the flat was on the upper floor
& it took the wrack-lunged doctor
                 as much as a half hour
                 to pause-puff up the steps

Miriam noticed how very yellow
                   his skin seemed to be
She thought, "Why are they taking so long fixing
             up that place so beautifully
             when it's killing him
                        to walk up the steps
             He'll be dead before he gets to use it."

        diabetes
            gout
             high blood pressure
                 liver prob's
                           congestive heart failure

        –thock thock thock

## A VISIT TO THE VA HOSPITAL

I was in New York City to plan the second annual
performance of the *New Amazing Grace*
and cabbed with the bard in the rain
                  up to the VA Hospital on 23rd
to visit Peter Orlovsky
                in a locked ward on the 17th floor

We had to pass through a metal detector
and get passes.  His ward had a buzzer door with the sign:
             Ring for Attendant
             Elopement Risk

During those years Peter looked like a combination of
Gustav Courbet & a 19th-century French farmer

but that late afternooon in his green hospital suit
he looked as glum as Leonardo's "Self-Portrait"
                              in the Royal Library in Turin

He had a hardbound copy of
*The Rise and Fall of the Third Reich*
                   on the visiting room table
He said he spiffled in his mind through
the WWII Nazi attack on Russia
to get himself calmed down to
sleep

          He was taking lithium & something called Tegretal
          The latter of which was giving him dyskinesia
          so they were giving him less
                        to lessen those effects

Peter didn't want to be there.
"Life has been no fun," he said.

I'd had many fine adventures over the years with Peter
beginning in '64
          when he and his brother Julius
          used to help collate the pages
          of *Fuck You/ A Magazine of the Arts*

I reminded him of the time we
went down with Neal in the VW van
to see Kesey in La Honda in '65.
I also mentioned the beautiful woman named Lydia
                    so smitten with him in '66

& I thought of other moments of fun
such as his thrilling descending yodel line
while playing the banjo
                back in '77 in Woodstock

He said he was going to resume his Buddhist practice.
Just as we left Allen pulled out a camera and took
some snaps of Peter & me

I asked what kind.
"It's an Olympus XA," he said.

I knew they weren't made anymore.
"You can get them,"
            said the ever-teaching teacher
"for about $150
        at K&M Camera
            on 23rd & 1st Avenue."

Not long thereafter I picked one up
at the very place he said they'd be

                •

        November 15, '95
        there was a second benefit
        performance of the *New Amazing Grace*

        Again the bard
            sang his trembling verses

        He told me afterwards
        that he had been weeping
                through the evening's final rounds

### DECEMBER 8
### BEAT CULTURE AND THE NEW AMERICA
### 1950–1965

There was an interesting show on the Beat Generation
                at the Whitney Museum
                    curated by Lisa Phillips
which opened on December 8

I bused down to the opening
It was a typically jittery NYC art crowd
as manic in '95
        as it was in '65 or '55

I'd never seen so much well-turned-out black attire
There must have been several million dollars' worth
                of fresh purchased noir!

A girl on a bench wearing wide black lipstick
    in the Whitney lobby
was frantically wave-drying
        her just-painted black fingernails
while a friend to her side in black sunglasses
          was chatting on a cell phone
—an image of an image as Plato described in the
        Allegory of the Cave.

Inside was a mighty flow of images!
Especially a glass topped case of
    William Burroughs' cut ups

& the manuscript of *On the Road*
        in a shrine-case

### DECEMBER 10
#### BEAT NIGHT AT THE WHITNEY

Then on Dec. 10th
there was a reading at the Whitney
A.G. with Steve Taylor,  and myself with Steve,
David Amram, Michael McClure w/ Ray Manzarek
& actor Keir Dullea reading
        Beat texts

Miriam and I were getting ready in Woodstock
to go to NYC for the reading

when Allen called early in the morning with bronchitis
and asked for Pavarotti's throat therapy

(A doctor friend of mine had helped restore
my voice before a Fugs reunion
    —he'd gotten the method from from Pav.'s dr.)

I read it to him:
    1. Take lots of liquids
    2. Squirt Vanceril down throat
           every ten minutes
    3. Don't talk
    4. Just before show time
      spray Afrin down throat

Then you can fully
croon.
It works.

We drove to NYC
to 437 East 12th, the bard's pad

where Steve & I rehearsed the Sappho poem
we'd sing in Greek at the Whitney

Allen was still weak.
Miriam didn't see how he could possibly perform
An accupuncturist & massagist were
working on him

yet somehow by show time
the bard was ready–

(it was the same with Gregory Corso
–backstage you might think
he could never go on
yet, like a Kennedy, he'd spring up
and press his lips to the mike
in full bard vitality)

A.G. performed the beautiful section
"Oh mother, what have I left out
Oh mother, what have I forgotten. . . ."
from "Kaddish"

and the fine pol-song  "Ballad of the Skeletons"
with Steve Taylor

It was in *The Nation* that week
Allen was less than pleased with the quality
of Calvin Trillin's political poems
*The Nation* published

so that "Ballad of the Skeletons"
was his answer lick
(to use a guitarist's term)
on what pol-poesy should be

> in the tradition of his "Capitol Air"
> "Hum Bomb" and "CIA Dope Calypso."
>
> (beginning around this time the bard,
> working with poets Andy Clausen & Eliot Katz
> began collecting pol-po's [political poems]
> from his friends
>           particularly on America's rightward drift.
> The pol-po's were to be published in a
>                 special section of *The Nation*)
>           The Whitney gave us a Town Car
>           for the trip back downtown
> with Corso announcing he'd support Colin Powell for pres.
> & A.G. heading
>           to a Harry Smith celebration at St. Mark's.
>           where they were rolling Harry's '53 3-D movie
>           called *Number 6*
>
>           & Miriam & I said good-bye to
>                 bard Corso & bard Ginsberg
>                       and drove back to Woodstock

# PART XXXIV

## 1996

> If you look at the Raw List
> of things he did
>           in the year before his
>                       death
> it's just about as complex
> as Beat Frenzy '56

> Ginsberg was determined to go the Thomas Hardy path:
> to write great poetry as he geezered

>                 •

> In February he played at the annual
> benefit for Tibet House at Carnegie Hall

In the audience was Danny Goldberg
then the president of Mercury Records
who had helped launch a spoken-word label called Mouth Almighty
(headed by Bill Adler & Bob Holman)

Allen sang "Ballad of the Skeletons"
& Goldberg offered to release it on Mercury/Mouth Almighty

•

In March the 'Zap
collaborated with Ornette Coleman
in a "poetry/jazz telecast" from Paris

He toured with Philip Glass
in France & the Czech Republic
doing portions of *Hydrogen Jukebox*

& he scarfed further moolah from
Retentia, the Muse of the Retained Image
from a photo show in Milan

•

I called Allen's office on April 10
The bard was in Texas
and there was bad news
about his congestive heart condition
a very serious situation

How about his new loft?
It won't be ready for a few months,
I was told.

On April 13, I chatted with Allen
He was back in his NY pad
and seemed okay

I wanted some more info on his '77 lunch with
CIA spook James Angleton
(for *1968, A History in Verse*)
&, as always,
he grabbed it out of his lobes
with not a missed beat

including some unfriendly remarks from the spy-sleaze
on Martin King
    (that the great American was "nothing but a
                whoremaster and a hypocrite")."

          ●

More good news from the muse Retentia in April
the bard went down to D.C. for readings
& a part in the National Portrait Gallery photo show
          "Rebel Poets & Painters of the 1950s"

In May there was the fine *Illuminated Poems*
          with illustrations by Eric Drooker
      from Four Walls Eight Windows

### BALLAD OF THE SK'S

May was the month they recorded "Ballad of the Skeletons"
w/ Lenny Kaye producing
Apparently they did a basic track and vocal
with Lenny on bass and Marc Ribot on guitar
          David Mansfield on guitar
The era of "mailing around the ADAT"
          for overdubs had long begun
so they forwarded an ADAT (digital 8-track tape)
to Philip Glass who laid down some piano

Then it was sent to Paul McCartney
      who put on a bunch of stuff
        including guitar, drums, an organ part & maracas

Mouth Almighty brought in Hal Willner
      known for his miracle mixes
      to work the faders, settings, pannings
          and knobs

"He took a little bit of bagginess out of the record"
          said Bill Adler
          o' Mouth Almighty

          ●

Jan Kerouac died on June 7 at 44
in Albuquerque the day after her spleen was removed
She had been on dialysis since '91
     the author of *Baby Driver* of '81
         *Trainsong* of '88  & she'd been working on *Parrot Fever*
          about her mother, Joan Haverty

         •

    His usual bard-in-residence
        for the summer session at Naropa
Then he spent ten days with Burroughs in Lawrence
taking pictures, and helping edit Burroughs' essay on
                 "Bureaucracy & Drugs"

In August
he read the Blake-thread "Sunflower Sutra"
to music by Philip Glass
& conducted by Yehudi Menhuin
       at Avery Fisher Hall, Lincoln Center

         •

On August 8 beat hero Herbert Huncke
     respected writer of tales
        passed away at 81
          at Beth Israel in NYC

    thock  thock

         •

In September the bard went on a
Buddhist retreat for ten days
with Gelek Rinpoche
      in Michigan

         •

On September 20 it was announced
that filmmaker Gus Van Sant
would direct a music video
      for "Ballad of the Skeletons"
Then, again at St. Mark's Church on October 8
there was a musical party for the bard's
*Selected Poems 1948-1995*
the release of "Ballad of the Skeletons"
& the thirtieth anniversary of the great Poetry Project

# Mixed-up Time-Travel

celebrating the Poetry Project's 30th Anniversary and
HarperCollins publication of *Allen Ginsberg's Selected Poems 1947-1995*

READINGS & PERFORMANCES by Allen Ginsberg with Art Baron
Kim Deal  Lenny Kaye  Tuli Kupferberg  Norm MacDonald
David Mansfield  Lenny Pickett  Colin Quinn  Lee
Ranaldo  Marc Ribot  Stephan Said  Ed Sanders  Steve
Shelley  Steven Taylor  Hal Willner  Garro Yellin
members of the Jazz Passengers & other special guests

8 PM Tuesday, October 8, 1996  St. Mark's Church in-the-Bowery

We had a quorum so we could call ourselves the Fugs
& we began with the core of our vision
Wm. Blake's "How Sweet I Roamed"
with the great David Mansfield on
                                        mandolin!

   I was surprised when the bard asked
   Tuli, Steve & me
   to include "River of Shit" in our set
      so I composed some new words for the bridge
      to fit the night

   & performed it with
   the all-star cats
      some from Sonic Youth
      & *Saturday Night Live.*

      People
      tend ne'er
      to speak
      in public
      of their rears or
      their daily
      visits to the
         porcelain vortex

but the bard who could
write brilliant pol-po's
and ruminative philosophical poems
                              to limn the age

          never let his audience
                    forget the vortex.

& so the Fugs roared forth with "Wide Wide River"
and the audience "caught fire" as they say
                    and roared along with us.

                              •

I was beginning to notice a memorial quality
in this string of salutes to the distinguished professor.

They seemed to me fueled by his obvious physical decline
these fetes for the 'Zap
                    in the '94-'95-'96 triad

They celebrated Chekhov
at the opening of *The Cherry Orchard*
                              in 1904

He could barely stand erect on stage
          rained upon with flowers
          and speeches of glorifications
                    from actors, journalists & the heads
                              of literary societies

          as if he were already gone

## THE NEW LOFT

He finally moved to his shiny new loft
                    in September o' '96

Peter would have the double apartment on East 12th
–he had originally been a cosigner of the lease
                    & so had legal claim under the
ever-crumbling NYC rent control rules
                    –in place since the rent struggles of World War II.

•

One of his final poems was a salute to his
                fast-voiced accompanist & arranger
                since '76  Steve Taylor
now on the faculty at Naropa, and married to Judy Hussie

Generous as ever the bard
                helped pay the maternity bills
                        for Steve & Judy's baby Eamonn
                                                born 12-3-96

## 1997

In February as in recent years the bard performed
                in an all-star Carnegie Hall benefit for Tibet House
                with Philip Glass, Michael Stipe, Natalie Merchant
                & Patti Smith.

## THE MTV SPECIAL

In his elegant loft
                appointed so well with light-hued wood
                fresh shiny floors
                        & un-catabolized white on the walls
the hourglass
                was doing what it does so well
& the fate shears
                were staring at the bard-thread.

I stayed there overnight on February 13
I'd taken part in a CD project with a bunch of recording artists
to lay down poems of Edgar Allan Poe
(I set to music the sonnet "To Helen"  & "The Haunted Palace"
                        from "The Fall of the House of Usher"
–I learned from the bard that Poe had been
                one of his first inspirations)

The CD was produced, as had been A.G.'s *The Lion for Real*
by Hal Willner & Michael Minzer
                for Mouth Almighty Records

After the sessions I headed for the loft
          on East 13th

    At last enough wall space for his art collection
    His records, books & CDs!

    I was glad that the great Bard
              had a pad with bowling alley bigness

    Along a wall past his piano and a pump organ
    was a spacious votivity zone–
    a prayer rug & cushions
    a cabinet & a table with candles
              & Buddhist relics

    beneath some tankas
        whose meaning he could trace
              with intricate tale
    & Trungpa's large "AH"
        on the wall of peace, love,
              acceptance, surrender.

    He showed me his guest room
    which sported a painting  by Paul McCartney
    & he took me into his bathroom
              to marvel at his bidet!
    The bathroom had its own window
        which looked out onto the loft
        toward the windows overlooking 14th Street!

    As weakened as he was
    he told me he had a new boyfriend
        and he was going to have his own
        MTV Unplugged!

I slept on a long white leather-covered couch
he assured me he'd gotten from the Salvation Army

*The Bard's Living Room with Salvation Army Couches*

His bed was at the other end of the wide-hearted loft
The light stayed on by his distant bed

in his nighttime habit
      of journals & verse

I heard the padding of slippers at 4 A.M.
through the high-vaulted loft
I looked up and agreed with Miriam
     how yellow his face skin shone
         as he passed in the hourglass silence

When we awakened
he offered a fresh rhubarb tart & rice milk,
        plus coffee & a hard-boiled egg
           for breakfast

Hal Willner came over
to talk about the A.G. MTV special scheduled for July 20
Allen was about as excited as I'd ever seen him
He said Dylan had agreed to do it,
plus the hot young singer named Beck, and Philip Glass
& he thought McCartney
     would come

He checked his blood, then shot up some insulin
        while we talked

He asked where he could get pump organs fixed
Even his little one was broken

I suggested doing a Net search for pump organ sites
–Bob Rosenthal agreed

I mentioned the big Victorian pump organ
                with the nice bass sound I'd borrowed
                back in '85 to write some arias
                                for an opera the Fugs were doing

I said we'd ship it from Woodstock
                        down to the loft
so that he or perhaps even Dylan, McCartney or Glass
could thunder-pump it for the Unplugged
                        (which we did)

He was going out to lunch with Bono of U2
Got dressed in his flower-tied finery
                On the kitchen windowsill
                was a goblet of pennies
                        next to the Tarot card for Justice

Ten days passed
& the great bard was feeling ever more fatigued so on February 23
Bob Rosenthal accompanied him all weak & unsteady
on the shuttle to Boston to see his cardiologist

On the flight A.G. read a poem from the night before
        called "Fame and Death"
        beginning "When I die
        I don't care what happens to my body . . ."

    It was then, in Boston I think, that his doctor
    asked him to go off all his various medications
        to try to focus on the cause
                of the tiredness.

## MARCH 4

    The bard left his sickbed in Boston
    to shuttle back to NYC
        in order to see Steve Taylor & Judy Hussie
        & new baby Eamonn
            in from Colorado for a visit.
    Aboard the plane
    he wrote a little rhymed poem "A fellow named Steven"
        (p. 73 in his final book, *Death & Fame*)

# PART XXXV

March 15 Gary Snyder called Ginsberg
Bob Rosenthal answered
who told him the diabetes, the heart murmur,
and various medications had joined
        to make the bard very very disoriented
                & fatigued

He called A.G. in the hospital
who told his old pal he'd been diagnosed
with a recurrence of hepatitis C
        "from years ago in India or Mexico.
He was so medicated that he wasn't able to
        talk very clearly,"
    Snyder later wrote.

•

When Allen was brought to Beth Israel
an emergency room doctor
handed him a poem
    asking for suggestions

and the frail poet complied on the spot!
made some notes on the page
    & the bard who wrote in Asclepiadeans
    improved the poem
    of the devotée of Asclepius

•

Of his final poems the most beautiful, to me
is the simple yet complex
    four-quatrain "Starry Rhymes"
at 4:51 A.M. on March 23, ending

      "Orion down
      North Star up
      Fiery leaves
      Begin to drop"

and then the next night
in tightly rhymed couplets
    "Thirty State Bummers"
his final political poem, a remarkable
    summation of the evil side
      of the American imperium
      it's secret wars, support for killer dictators

    with doublets such as
      "Richard Helms Angleton live
      we were lucky to survive"

    We WERE lucky
      to survive these oppressionists

•

March 27 at 2:29 A.M. in the hospital
    "w/ dangerous hepatitis C" in the bard's words
he awakened from a dream
that he'd had a baby

and there was a "glow of happiness next morn,
        warm glow of pleasure half the day"

•

    He phoned the world
            in cordless profusion
probably made 500 calls
          maybe more

    A.G. called Gary late at night in Nevada City
    He'd just been diagnosed
          with the teminality
    He had two to five
    Gary said he'd come to NYC for a visit in a few weeks
    and the call sank to silence with A.G.'s sob

•

He called Steve Taylor in Boulder:
". . . the doctor came in and I said well what's the news
and he said not good and I said cancer and he said yes.  And I
said any operation or remedy . . . and he said no . . . They gave me
four to five months . . . But I've been weakening, I can tell,
and I think maybe only one or two . . . I was amazed how calm I was . . .
Some kind of equanimity—must have been all those years
               of Buddhist lectures, sitting . . ."
Taylor asked if he should fly to NYC before the Fugs went to Italy
He said "No, carry on,"
      Taylor could visit after the tour, and
          maybe they could do some recording

Taylor asked if the bard had any new songs and he sang:

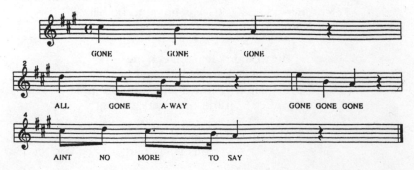

Steve Taylor sent us a note
       that Allen was in the hospital

Right away I called Allen's # in NYC
& reached Peter Hale
          longtime staff member
who sketched out the bitter truth:
"He has liver cancer
There are so many nodes there's
no way to pick it out–
a liver transplant is out of the question

He's making a lot of calls
       & writing furiously."

      •

How many phone calls?  Maybe a thousand?
To Dylan, McCartney, boyfriends, girlfriends,
relatives, writers
       & a long sad tearful call to Burroughs.

To Hal Willner he said
"Sorry for not doing the Unplugged"
He suggested Hal check out the 25 hours of
tapes from the Knitting Factory in '95

      •

That afternoon, March 30, the bard called Woodstock
        & spoke with Miriam
Peter Orlovsky, he said, was going to be his
      attendant

("He wouldn't leave me alone
if I were sick in bed, dying,
grey-haired . . . he'd have pity on me,"
      the bard said long ago

and he recalled how carefully Peter had cared for
      his failing father Oleg back in '82)

He assured Miriam he was not in pain
He'd finished his book
& he would be receiving guests at home.

He told her of the dream
                wherein he'd had a child
and awakened very happy
It was the day, he said, they'd
                        given him the bad news

He asked how Miriam was
& wanted to be remembered to our daughter Deirdre
He said he wasn't afraid

She said, "We love you."
He replied, "I know."

                   •

A few hours later
                when Miriam described the call from Allen
I dialed him at the hospital
He was having a meeting with Bob Rosenthal
                        and  couldn't talk long

He said he'd finished his book
                & was signing some photos

The perils of his illness, however,
were not so great
as to stop the
                famous PR instincts of the bard
–he was afraid I was going
to break the story of his
                terminal illness
                        in the *Woodstock Journal*
"Don't write about it in the *Journal*,"
"Of course I won't," I replied.

"I'll send you a new poem,"  he said.

The bard with maybe a 25-page press list
& the keenest sense of ink since Whitman
                      wanted to coordinate one more release

"OK honey," he said
"See you in a while
Love you."

•

Among the calls were those to wealthy friends
asking them to keep up their support,
say to Naropa
                or to Gregory

"This is great!"
                he exclaimed to Bob Rosenthal
"I'm dying, & no one can
                        say no!"

He was trying to reach George Soros
whose Christmas parties he attended
                                to ask for help
but couldn't get through.

Maybe the 'Zap could have gotten Mr. Soros
to fund the much-needed
                Golden Bard Retirement Home network!

## PART XXXVI

They brought him home on Wednesday, April 2
                to the light-wood-hued
                        loft with his books & paintings

& set up his final encampment

They placed a hospital bed near the
                white-bearded photo of Whitman
                        on a white brick wall
                                between two windows that looked
                                        upon 14th Street

•

There were plans to bring in portable
      recording equipment
  and possibly try to do his MTV special
                               from his resting place

     Peter Orlovsky was there
     helping him into his pajamas

     It was around then, w/ Shelley Rosenthal's help
     that they made a mighty
     fish-head health stew on the stove
     with all kinds of shellfish & restorative items
                          tossed aboard

     Wednesday night he listened to his final music
     Ma Rainey's "See See Rider"
         and they brought down a blues text
     from his well-ordered walls
             so he could sing along

•

Miriam & I were at the *Woodstock Journal* office
that night late
getting the paper out before we
         flew off to Italy for Fugs reunions

so we missed a message from the bard. First a cough,
then a weak voice, "This is Allen Ginsberg. It's
Wednesday night, 10 or 10:30. I'm out of the hospital
and back home. I think the last time I talked to you
I was too tired to say much, but I'm home now.
So you call, you know, lunchtime 12:30 or 1:30."

### THURSDAY, APRIL 3

     The next day A.G. was fairly alert
     coming up with instructions for the next few weeks
     and settling in for a multi-month Hey Jude fade

     He was on the phone with Nanda Pivano
     from Italy, one of his finest translators,
     when he started to throw up

Rosenthal told her he'd have to hang up.
& the bard said he wanted to go to sleep.

He'd written a letter to Bill Clinton
which noted he was sending some poems
            but he'd not gotten to choose them

●

That afternoon before we left for Newark International
I called but they said he was asleep
            It must have been after that terrible  moment
                    on the phone with Nanda Pivano.

### FRIDAY, APRIL 4

Night came and then morn
& both Bob Rosenthal & Bill Morgan were worried
came early to the loft

Peter was not there
He had gone out
and purchased a hot bicycle.

Bob went in to awaken the bard
to see what they should do
but he could not be roused

They even went so far as to give a pinch
        but the genius so easy to be awake slept fast

They called the hospice doctor
who quickly came
            & judged he'd suffered a stroke in the night
had just a few hours to live

The staff called the family
& his brother Eugene & family arrived
                            late in the morning

●

The Fugs were in Milan
but Steve Taylor called the loft to get filled in
We'd just returned to our hotel
from a rehearsal place
        along a canal designed
        by Leonardo da Vinci

when we heard about the stroke
Bill Morgan said that
        the end was very near.

We shared a loaf of olive bread
then opened some liquor
        and held our glasses high, clinked them,
        "Here's to the soul of Allen Ginsberg."

## TURN TURN TURN
## (TROPÉ TROPÉ TROPÉ)

Voice to voice to voice
by e, by fax, by phone, by street-stop
        the word spread worldly

& I heard there were satellite trucks
with their focusing dishes outside the building

The loft filled with friends
Old pals gathered in quiet grief

There were Peter Orlovsky, Rani Singh, Shelley Rosenthal
(& her and Bob's two sons Aliah and Isaac)
Francesco and Alba Clemente
Philip Glass, Patti Smith and her daughter,
Oliver Ray, Andrew Wylie
Larry Rivers came down from his loft above
Roy Lichtenstein, Raymond Foye
Gregory Corso,
        George & Anna Condo &  many others

They went to sit beside him
hold his hand,
        whisper a message,
                kiss him, weep

•

Andrew Wylie later said
"I certainly worshiped him
I thought he was a great man
He had this amazing effect on me
I always felt good for a day and a half
                    after seeing him."

Wylie put his words on an important
part of the bard:
            the good feelings lasting days
                        from interactions

•

        Gelek Rinpoche flew in from Michigan
        He and other monks
        chanted and prayed
                by the bard's extensive
                sitting zone & altar in the midroom.

•

Allen's cousin and doctor, Joel Gaidemak
was on hand as was a hospice nurse
                    to administer morphine

Two narrow tubes went up to his nose
                    with oxygen

Joel lived upstate, and the bard over the years
had "counted on his opinion a lot
                    in medical matters"
                Bill Morgan later said

He was the kind of doctor, far too rare,
who would actually explain things
                    in bard-mind depth

•

Everybody was aware of the bard's
photos of the dying Julian Beck & his uncle Abe Ginsberg
so the delicate issue of photos arose
A few went out to purchase cameras.

Corso wanted a picture with Allen
He crouched by the death cot
                    with his arm over the bard
            while someone took a snap
            with a toss-away Woolworth's camera

(Oddly too that evening all of Corso's books,
signed over to the bard
                    from all those years
            somehow vanished
            from the pad)


                    •


A friend who was there told me of one
        of the bard's young pals
        sitting on the death bed
                    his back to Ginsberg
laughing and chatting


                    •


            At last the quiet grieving day departed.
            They sent out for food
            and late in the evening many left
            –his brother, weeping and
                            saying good-bye
            Gregory, others.

            and then about 2 A.M.
            people sacked out here and there


                    •


It was said his face perked up
                    toward the end
how the stress-lines smoothed
"I had never seen him so handsome,"
            wrote Rosebud Pettet
            in her careful
                    memoir of those hours

●

The artist George Condo
　　　made some sketches
　　　　　　for a painting
　　　　　　　　which the bard had said was okay

●

Old friend Rosebud Pettet
　　　sat stroking his feet

the bard attired in a Jewel Heart T-shirt
frailer and skinner than any had seen

but his face showed peace
　　　　　　　　to Rosebud closely looking

His breathing slowing down to 20
　　　　　　　　　　19, 18 per minute

And then at 2:40 A.M.
　　　Saturday morn
　　　　　　4-5-97
　　　　　　　　he seemed to try to sit up

and then his diamond brain ceased being served.

Thus left earth
the bard called Allen Ginsberg
whom so many of us loved

the Lion faced one
　　　in the long Egyptian boat
　　　　　　　no doubt getting
　　　　　as close to Osiris
　　　　　　　　& the sun disk
　　　　　　　as he can

Buddha singing one
　　　on a blue Tara raft

Kaddish chanting one
　　　　　on a boat made of stone

Fun shouting one
        on a boat made of froth

Pain relieving one
        on a boat made of sighs

•

People were asked to give space
& touch him not till
certain prayers and inductions were performed.

His body was cordoned off for hours
as Gelek Rinpoche & the lamas
prayed and chanted

–there was something about
waiting till his cheeks
had sunk in a certain way
plus I think they had to grant the bard some initiations
which he had not had a chance to receive

All through Saturday they sat and chanted
till finally Bob Rosenthal called the
midnight squad from the morgue
who zipped the phantom all skinny
in a body bag

Peter Orlovsky
at the bed's foot
hands pressed together
& bowing at the zip
Thus went back toward sunshine
the great bard Allen Ginsberg
O float on the wave just a bit more, bard flower

                –EDWARD SANDERS
                *March 1997-December 1999*

# AFTERWORD

## THE POETRY & LIFE OF ALLEN GINSBERG

I did not plan to write a book on Allen Ginsberg, but rather an extended elegy, which I began at the time of his death in April 1997 when for a while grief seemed to course without limit. I would be walking down the street and suddenly weep thinking about him. After a while, I decided that maybe silent mourning was the proper route, and decided to abandon the inch or so of notes I had made for the elegy.

In September of that year, I taught a course called "The Poetry & Life of Allen Ginsberg" at the Schule für Dichtung in Vienna. To prepare, I created a fairly thick three-ring notebook which included a history I put together of his life. In 1998 I decided to run some of that notebook in the *Woodstock Journal*. There was a favorable response from readers, so I kept publishing the notes, polishing them and adding new sections till it became obvious that a book was forming.

The life of Allen Ginsberg was very complicated, so *The Poetry & Life of Allen Ginsberg* is really a kind of pathway through the Forest Ginsberg, and because it is a pathway I have had to leave out a great many interesting anecdotes, events and interactions. Allen's soul was such a great and positive beacon that he attracted literally thousands of people who felt close to him. Inevitably, this walkway through the Forest Ginsberg could not touch a number of important connections in his life, and I ask for the indulgence of those poets, activists, filmmakers, musicians, family members, painters, Beat Generation scholars, & friends in countries all around the world, who had their own complicated relationships with the great bard Allen Ginsberg, and whose memories are not heard and seen along this pathway.

There are two good biographies of Allen Ginsberg, *Dharma Lion*, by Michael Schumacher, and *Ginsberg*, by Barry Miles. If they are read together, each with its slightly different point of view, Allen Ginsberg emerges as the great human that he was. His journals, his multitudinous interviews, his poems (always autobiographical), the endnotes to his books, his descriptions of his photos, and my own files, including many clippings, journals, letters and tapes from my own numerous interactions, performances and capers with him for thirty-four years, were helpful in creating this book. The memories of my wife Miriam, and of Bob Rosenthal, Bill Morgan, Raymond Foye, Rosebud Pettet, Steve Taylor, Andrew Wylie, Hal Willner, Bill Adler and others were very helpful, and I am very grateful for them.

I loved him, and he is in my mind almost as if he were alive even as I type this on a warm spring day, wishing he were staying across the street at Raymond Foye's house (as he sometimes did) so I could go over there for a chat (and some good advice, for he was a teacher around the clock).

He kept everything—doodles on napkins, the 60,000 letters of friends, the 18,900 pages (and more) of journals, and just about every fragment of his time-track, so it might be interesting for someone to do a Total Biography of Ginsberg. He seemed to be asking for it with his tens of thousands of photos, his thousands of recordings and interviews, so perhaps a day-by-day bio, maybe 25,000 pages long, is what is required. That would be a Joycean endeavor. On the other hand, his final ten years would make a fine project for a biographer.

I cannot be the one, but I have written a temporary path, with log bridges over streams and ropes down cliff sides, through the Forest Ginsberg, for your study and enjoyment.

—Edward Sanders
*Woodstock, New York*

## POETRY BOOKS

*Death & Fame  Last Poems 1993-1997*. HarperCollins, NYC, 1999.
*Selected Poems* 1947-1995. HarperCollins, NYC, 1996.
*Illuminated Poems*. Illustrated by Eric Drooker. Four Walls Eight Windows, NYC 1996.
*Howl Annotated* w/facsimile manuscript. HarperPerennial, NYC, 1995.

*Cosmopolitan Greetings, Poems 1986-1993.* HarperCollins, NYC, 1994.
*White Shroud, Poems 1980-1985.* Harper & Row, NYC, 1986.

*Collected Poems, 1947-1980.* HarperCollins, NYC, 1984.
*Plutonian Ode, Poems 1977-1980.* City Lights Books, SF, 1982.

*Mind Breaths, Poems 1971-76.* City Lights Books, SF, 1978.
*Iron Horse.* Coach House Press, Toronto/City Lights Books, SF, 1974.
*The Fall of America, Poems of These States.* City Lights Books, SF, 1973.
*The Gates of Wrath, Rhymed Poems 1948-1951.* Four Seasons, Bolinas, 1972.
*Planet News.* City Lights Books, SF, 1968.
*Reality Sandwiches.* City Lights Books, SF, 1963.
*Kaddish and Other Poems.* City Lights Books, SF, 1961.
*Howl and Other Poems.* City Lights Books, SF, 1956.

## PROSE BOOKS

*Deliberate Prose – Selected Essays.* HarperCollins, NYC, 2000.
*Luminous Dreams.* Zasterle Press, Gran Canaria, 1997.
*Indian Journals.* Grove Press, NYC, 1996.
*Journals Mid-Fifties.* HarperCollins, NYC, 1995.
*Journals Early Fifties Early Sixties.* Ed. G. Ball, Grove Press, NYC, 1977, 1993.
*Your Reason and Blake's System.* Hanuman Books, NYC, 1988.
*Straight Hearts' Delight: Love Poems and Selected Letters.* With Peter Orlovsky, Gay Sunshine Press, SF, 1980.
*Composed on the Tongue.* (Literary Conversations, 1967-1977). Grey Fox Press, Bolinas, 1980.
*As Ever: Collected Correspondence Allen Ginsberg & Neal Cassady.* Creative Arts, Berkeley, 1977.
*To Eberhart from Ginsberg.* Penmaen Press, Lincoln, MA, 1976.
*Chicago Trial Testimony.* City Lights Trashcan of History Series #1, SF, 1975.
*The Visions of the Great Rememberer* (Epilogue to Kerouac's *Visions of Cody*). Penguin, NYC, 1993.
*Allen Verbatim: Lectures on Poetry etc.* Ed. Gordon Ball. McGraw Hill, NYC, 1974. (op)
*Gay Sunshine Interview* (with Allen Young). Grey Fox Press, Bolinas, 1974.

*The Yage Letters* (with William Burroughs). City Lights Books, SF, 1963.

## PHOTOGRAPHY BOOKS & CATALOGS

*Allen Ginsberg 108 Images.* Fred Hoffman Fine Art, Santa Monica, 1995.

*Snapshot Poetics.* Chronicle Books, SF, 1993.

*Allen Ginsberg Photographs.* Twelvetrees Press, 1991.

*Reality Sandwiches: Fotografien.* Nishen, Berlin, West Germany, 1989.

*Allen Ginsberg Fotografier 1947-1987.* Forlaget Klim, Arhus, Denmark, 1987.

*Allen Ginsberg & Robert Frank.* Galerie Watari, Tokyo, Japan, 1985.

## ANTHOLOGIES, INTERVIEWS, ESSAYS, BIBLIOGRAPHIES, PHOTO CAHIERS

*The Works of Allen Ginsberg, 1941-1994, A Descriptive Bibliography.* Bill Morgan, Greenwood Press, Westport, 1995.

*Dharma Lion: A Critical Biography of Allen Ginsberg.* Michael Schumacher, St. Martin's Press, NYC, 1992.

*The Portable Beat Reader,* Ann Charters, ed., Viking Portable Library, NYC, 1992.

*Allen Ginsberg: A Biography.* Barry Miles, Simon & Schuster, NYC, 1989.

*Best Minds A Tribute to Allen Ginsberg.* Bill Morgan and Bob Rosenthal, eds., Lospecchio Press, NYC, 1986.

*On the Poetry of Allen Ginsberg.* Lewis Hyde, ed., University of Michigan Press, Ann Arbor, 1984.

*Dear Allen: Letters to Allen Ginsberg.* William S. Burroughs, Full Court Press, NYC. 1982.

*The Post -Moderns: The New American Poetry* Revised. D. Allen & G. Butterick, Grove Press, NYC, 1982.

*Allen Ginsberg Bibliography 1969-1978.* M. Kraus, The Scarecrow Press, Inc., Metuchen, NJ, 1980.

*Talking Poetics from Naropa Institute.* Waldman and Webb, eds., Shambhala, Boulder, CO, Vol. 1-1978, Vol. 2-1979.

*Visionary Poetics of Allen Ginsberg.* Paul Portuges, Ross-Erikson, Santa Barbara, 1978.

*The New Naked Poetry.* Berg & Mazey, eds., Bobbs-Merrill, NYC, 1976.

*The Beat Book.* A. & G. Knight, eds., California, PA, 1974.
*The Poetics of the New American Poetry.* Allen & Tallman, eds., Grove Press, NYC, 1973.
Allen Ginsberg Bibliography 1943-1967. G. Dowden, ed., City Lights Books, SF, 1971.
*Scenes Along the Road.* Ann Charters, ed., Gotham Book Mart, NYC, 1970. Reprint City Lights, SF,1984.
*Playboy.* Interview w. Paul Carrol, Chicago, April 1969.
*The Poem in Its Skin.* Paul Carrol, ed., Big Table/Follet, Chicago, 1968.
*Paris Review Interviews.* With Tom Clark. 3rd Series, Viking, NYC, 1967.
*The Marihuana Papers.* D. Solomon, ed., Bobbs-Merrill, NYC, 1966.
*A Casebook of the Beat.* T. Parkinson, ed., Thos. Y. Crowell, NYC, 1961.
*The New American Poetry 1945-1960.* Don Allen, ed., Grove Press, NYC, 1960.

## CDS & PHONOGRAPH RECORDS: POETRY

*Howl & Other Poems.* Fantasy Records, 1998.
*Jack Kerouac Mexico City Blues.* 242 Poems read by Allen Ginsberg; Shambhala Pubs Audio, Boston, 1996.
*The Ballad of the Skeletons.* With Paul McCartney, Philip Glass, Produced by Lenny Kaye, Mouth Almighty/Mercury, 1996.
*Howl, U.S.A.* Lee Hyla score, Kronos Quartet, Nonesuch, 1996.
*The Lion for Real.* Produced by Hal Willner, Mouth Almighty/Mercury, 1989, 1996.
*Holy Soul Jelly Roll: Poems & Songs 1949 -1993.* 4-CD set, produced by Hal Willner, Rhino Records, 1994.
*Hydrogen Jukebox.* Music by Philip Glass, libretto by Allen Ginsberg, Elektra Nonesuch #979286-2, 1993.
*Cosmopolitan Greetings Jazzy Opera.* Music by George Gruntz, words by Allen Ginsberg, 2-CD set, Migros-Genossenschafts-Bund Muzikscene Schweitz MG BCD9203, Postfach 266 CH-8031 Zürich, Switzerland, 1993.
*Howls, Raps & Roars.* Recordings from the San Francisco Poetry Renaissance, includes "Howl and Other Poems," 4FCD-4410-2 Fantasy Records, 1993.
*Made in Texas.* 2 songs ("Airplane Blues" and Blake's "Nurses Song"), c/o Michael Minzer, Paris Records, 7010 Desco Sq., Dallas, TX 75225, 1986.

*First Blues: Songs.* Produced by John Hammond 1975-1981, John Hammond Records, NY 1983. (op)

*Birdbrain, with the Gluons.* Single, Wax Trax, 638 E. 13 Ave., Denver, CO, 80203, 1981. (op)

*First Blues, A.G. on Harmonium.* Recorded by Harry Smith, ed. A. & S. Charters, Folkways Records.

FSS 37560, NYC, 1981. In Print c/o Smithsonian Institute, 955 l'Enfant Plaza, Washington D.C. 20560; cassette order department: 301-443-2314/fax: 443-1819

Giorno Poetry Systems (G.P.S. 008-9, 016-7, 018-19) 1975-1980, G.P.S. Institute 222 Bowery, NYC, 10012.

*Gate, 2 Evenings with Allen Ginsberg.* The Loft, 1001 Stereo, Munich, 1980. Distributed 2001, Frankfurt; by City Lights, USA. (op)

*Wm. Blake's Songs of Innocence & of Experience.* Tuned by A.G., M-G-M Records, NY, 1970 FTS 3083. (o.p.)

*Kaddish.* Atlantic Verbum Series 4001, NYC, 1966. (o.p.)

*Howl and Other Poems.* Fantasy-Galaxy Records, #7013, 2600 10th St Berkeley, CA, 94710, 1959.

*Hobo Blues Band.* Hungarian production. Budapest.

*Naropa Institute Tape Archive* - 20 Naropa Poetry readings, including performances with music from 1974-1988. Send for catalog: 2130 Arapahoe Ave, Boulder, CO, 80302.

## FILMS/VIDEOS

*A Poet on the Lower East Side.* Gyula Gazdag, 1997. A.G. with Istvan Eorsi & friends walking the Village telling stories. Contact GGAZDAG@EMELNITZ.UCLA.EDU.

*The Ballad of the Skeletons.* Music video, directed by Gus Van Sant, Mouth Almighty/Mercury, 1996.

*The Life and Times of Allen Ginsberg.* Produced by Jerry Aronson, 1993. First Run Features, 153 Waverly Place, NYC, 10014; 212-243-0600/fax: 212-989-7649.

*Paul Bowles: The Complete Outsider.* Produced & directed by Catherine Warnow & Regina Weinreich, 1993; First Run Features, 153 Waverly Place, NYC, 10014. Appearances.

*Evening with Allen Ginsberg.* With Don Was, bass, Lannan Foundation, 5401 McConnell Ave., LA, CA, 90066, 1990. Good performance video, some conversation.

*Growing Up in America.* Cinephile, Ltd. 508 Queen Street West, 3rd Floor, Toronto, Ontario, Canada, M5V 2B3, 416-368-7499. Directed by Morley Markson, 1988. Small interview.

*It Don't Pay to Be an Honest Citizen.* 78 min. color, 1984. Object Productions/Jacob Burckhardt, 201 E. 4th Street, NYC, 10009. Bit part.

*Voices & Visions.* Series on Modern American Poetry in 13 one-hour segments, Jan. 1988 PBS broadcast. Allen Ginsberg appears in the segments on Whitman and W. C. Williams. Available in video cassette and 16-mm film through NY Cente. for Visual History, 625 Broadway, NYC 10012, 212-777-6900. Comment on W.C.W.

*Beat Generation.* Renaissance Motion Pictures, 23 W. 73rd St., Suite #101, NYC, 10023. 212-496 0088. Produced by Janet Forman, 1987. Appearances.

*What Happened to Kerouac.* 96 minutes, 1985. Directed by Richard Lerner & Lewis MacAdams, a Richard Lerner Production, New Yorker Films, 16 W. 61st St., NYC, 10023, 212-247-6110. Appearances.

*Father Death Blues.* Part of "Don't Grow Old," for the Manhattan Video Project, Out There Productions, Inc., 156 W. 27th St., Suite 5-W, NYC, 10001, 1984. 4-minute music poetry video.

*Burroughs The Movie.* Directed by Howard Brookner, produced by Howard Brookner and Alan Yentob.Giorno Video Pak 2, VHS GPS 034. © 1983 Citifilmsworks, © (p) 1985 Giorno Poetry Systems Institute Inc., 222 Bowery, NYC, 10012. Appearances..

*Writers In Conversation #16.* Allen Ginsberg with R.D. Laing, ICA Video, London, Dist. Roland Collection, 3120 Pawtucket Rd. Northbrook, Il, 60602, 1985. Performance.

*Allan 'N' Allen's Complaint.* 30-minute color video, Nam June Paik & Shigeko Kubota. Appeared at 1983 Whitney Museum Biennial. Dist. by Send Video Arts, 1250 17th St., San Francisco, CA, 94110. Interesting feature.

*Poetry in Motion.* 87 minutes, produced and directed by Ron Mann, 1982. Sphinx Productions in association w/Giorno Poetry Systems, 222 Bowery, NYC. Distributed by Giorno Poetry Systems. Includes "Bird Brain," "Do the Meditation," Capital Air" and an interview with Ginsberg. Bit part, not good.

*The Living Tradition: Ginsberg on Whitman.* Full-color Sound Filmstrip with addit. cassette and teacher's guide. Jr. High-Jr. Coll. CE392 (The Liv. Tradition—2 cassettes.) Single cassette: *Ginsberg Reads Whitman.* Dist: Centre Productions Inc, 1312 Pine, Suite A, Boulder, CO, 80302.

*Fried Shoes, Cooked Diamonds.* With Corso, Burroughs, Leary, Orlovsky, Waldman. Directed by Constanzo Allione. Dist. Mystic Fire Video, 24 Horatio St. #3, NYC, 10014.

*Renaldo & Clara.* 2- & 4-hr. versions. Dir. Bob Dylan, Rolling Thunder Review stars. Distributed by Circuit Films, 910 Hennepin, Mpls, MN, 55403. 1977. 4th lead role. (op)

*Me & My Brother.* Directed by Robert Frank with Orlovsky Brothers, Joe Chaikin, NYC, 1966. Distributed as below.

*Pull My Daisy.* Directed by Robert Frank & A. Leslie, narrated by Jack Kerouac with Corso, Orlovsky, Rivers and Amram. NYC, Dist. Houston Museum of Art, 1958.

## ARCHIVES

Green Library
Standord University
Standford, CA 94305-6004

## ONWARDNESS

Allen Ginsberg Trust
Box 582 Stuyvesant Station
New York, NY 10009